THE
VALENTINE
PROPHECIES

DAVID DELLIT

THE VALENTINE PROPHECIES

Published by Exodus Design Christian Book Publishing

ISBN: 978-1495316623

First Edition: February 2014

Editing and Proofreading by Christian Editing Services
www.christianeditingservices.org

Book Cover Design by Exodus Design Studios
www.ExodusDesign.com

Back Cover Photo by Peter Williams of Turning Heads Photography
www.turningheads.com.au

TABLE OF CONTENTS

SECTION 1
THE VALENTINE PROPHECIES

SECTION 2
HOW TO GET CLOSER TO GOD

SECTION 3
WHY ARE WE PRAYING FOR BUT NOT SEEING REVIVAL

PREFACE

On Valentine's Day 2013, I had an unusual but enlightening experience with God. I was anointed and instructed by God to write down what he gave me and then to send it out. Christ desires to return swiftly but his bride, the church, is not ready; none of us are ready. The last of the last days are upon us. God instructs us on how to spiritually thrive, not just survive, and teaches us how to use his words and his power to transform ourselves and others, to transform Christ's church, and to transform his kingdom worldwide. It is time for the church to wake from her slumber. Christ's return is imminent and God calls us to transform and reform so that his planned worldwide revival can begin and the radiant bride of Christ, his church, will be ready for Christ's return.

This is the beginning of one of the most exciting times for Christ's church but we must do everything under the guidance of the Holy Spirit, in his love, and by his power. Some of his words are corrective but his love for us shines through. On average, in the western world, regular Christian worshippers account for only 3% to 5% of the population, an almost insignificant minority of our societies. God has plans for his church to explode—by his power and in his love. By anointing me to receive his words on Valentine's Day, God was signalling his intention to bring us into a romantic and passionate relationship with him. For those of you who know the voice of the Holy Spirit, he will confirm for you that this book contains words for you from God. For those who do not know his voice, I pray that a spirit of conviction will come upon you as you read.

God challenges all believers in God with the warning that he is sending Jesus very soon and, for those who will not listen, who are not caught up with Christ, but are left behind, "…the earth will descend into a hellish state." These late-comer believers will sadly repent as martyrs. God is warning us now so that we may all listen and escape these terrors soon to fall upon the earth.

I

ACKNOWLEDGEMENTS

I thankfully acknowledge:

The hands-on work of God the Father, of the Lord Jesus Christ, and of the Holy Spirit poured into '*The Valentine Prophecies*,' because without them this book would not exist.

My beautiful wife who I love and laugh with, who together with God is one of the strands in our three-strand marriage-cord.

My precious daughter who expresses so much pride in me that it leaves me wondering what I can possibly be doing to deserve it.

My hilarious granddaughter with whom I love to swim, box, wrestle, chase, play dolls, and cuddle, and who can make me feel both very young and very old at the very same time.

My friend Pete Williams who is like a spiritual rock from God, and who along with his wife Jenny, believed from the beginning that '*The Valentine Prophecies*' is from God.

My friends Anne and Paul Hilliar from my home church whose advice, encouragement, and assistance in multiple aspects of this book has brought me much strength.

This book bears the Doris Schuster touch, which is so much more than that of a consummate professional Editor and Proofreader. The Doris touch cannot easily be separated from the touch of the Holy Spirit, because together they took this book and further refined it like a potter polishing a precious vessel. www.christianeditingservices.org

God entrusted to Exodus Design the cover design, the book layout, and the web design. More than amazingly gifted professionals, their spiritual sensitivity to God's guiding hand, resulted in their work perfectly reflecting the spirit of God's message in '*The Valentine Prophecies*.' www.exodusdesign.com

INTRODUCTION

Arguably, the best and most polite two words to describe what I have done here are *SHAMELESS AUDACITY* (borrowed from the Senior Pastor at the church where I worship). I humbly claim to be a man called by God to write down his words as he placed his thoughts into my mind. I typed them and kept on typing until God finished saying all that he had to say. This happened over a period of months and the delivery dates are indicated above each section.

I expect to be labelled a liar by many. Nevertheless, like most believers in God, if personally asked by God to do something, I do it—or at least I try to do it, whether the result brings applause or persecution. Although the last 30 years have been punctuated by powerful acts of God in my life, and I, as well as others, have thought that I was receiving a powerful calling, I did not know what my calling was until God revealed it to me earlier this year (2013).

I am compelled to type God's thoughts and send this out, for there is a restless burning within me that will not go away. It drives me on to complete the task God has given me and to complete it swiftly. I am deeply humbled to be called and anointed by God to write down his words for his people.

There are some in Christ's kingdom whose ministries are thriving on the Holy Spirit's power, but most are languishing at best, or even failing. God expresses his frustration as he corrects some of us— particularly those of us who are keen to correct others—but his call is driven by his love for all his children. God bares his heart to us and shares his innermost feelings. Those who are closer to God will encounter God's joy and God's sorrow. Overall, God's letter is positively exciting as he powerfully calls us into the last of the last days. Because he chose Valentine's Day (a celebration of love) as the day of my anointing, I believe that the words from God in this book are meant to be a modern-day "love letter" from God to each one of us.

To be everything God always intended us to be in his kingdom, we need help. To be his radiant bride, we need help. To be his champion, we need help. God has given us the most professional help in the form of our guide and mentor, the Holy Spirit, who knows the truth and the way. All we have to do is ask, listen to him, and desire to follow his instructions, and we will receive his advice, his encouragement and his correction. With the Holy Spirit at our side, we are led into the full victory that Christ died to give us, both the everyday victory and the eternal victory.

If you can hear God's voice, he will confirm for you that this book contains his words, his thoughts, his plans, and his feelings for you.

In the section "A Word from the Messenger", I included some of the incidents that caused me to realise that God was trying to catch my attention.

At the end of the book, you will find a list of churches, ministries, and ministers that God has used to help me grow in my faith. None are perfect, but most possess a God-given quality that blesses the kingdom, encourages the saints, and glorifies God and Christ.

BEFORE MY CALLING
AND ANOINTING

Saturday, February 2, 2013

I asked God, "Father, what is my gift?" " God replied gently, "Writing. You already know that." "What should I write and when should I write it?" I asked. "Son, I want you to show them relationship. The one we have together. But not only that, I want you to tell them how I think and feel today. Many talk about my Word as if they know, and they don't; but you are not only gifted to write, but also to listen and to hear me share. I want you to write what you hear and share it with them, share it with the world."

"You mean how to get close to you and how to overcome sin?" I asked. "Yes, but not just that, David; I want you to write about what I consider to be the highs and the lows in the church today, and how long the earth has before I send my Son, the Lord Jesus Christ, to end this age and to destroy the universe."

"Father, I expect that trouble will come to me by writing this book for you," I said. "Yes David," God replied, "Many will scoff at you and call you mad or a liar; others will say you are expressing your opinion and will hate you. Still others will know you are right, but hate you anyway, out of jealousy. A few will love you for my words. These will be those who ask me if what you are writing is from me and, when I confirm it for them, will treasure this writing because it is from me to them, to help them live to please me more in these modern and last days. Trouble or no trouble, I expect you to write what I say. Those who have a heart for me will hear and will be richly blessed."

My mind began to ponder what I had just heard. Then God interrupted my thoughts with these words, "Son, let me speak." I saw a swirling, smoky vapour that was dull with little light. It was vast in size so that, when I looked inside, it seemed to go on and on. And God, said, "How many people think of God as a vapour, as a swirling, floating vapour far off, with no personality, no thoughts, no feelings, no opinions, no voice, and not able to see and hear the amount of rubbish that is lived and spoken and held up as truth—complete and useless rubbish. It is as if this age thinks it has all the time in the world, but it has not." "How long do we have, Father?" "Much less time than you think, David. People live as if they have millennia, but the time is short, very short. It is time for you and for everyone to wake up, for I am sending my Son soon, very soon. These are the end times; the end of the end times.

"I know the hearts that are laughing as they read this, David—and there are many—but on that day, those who are not ready will not be laughing. On that day, the only ones happy of heart will be those instantly finding themselves to be with the Lord, knowing what has happened and knowing they were found worthy. Many who feel confidence in being ready today will, in fact, be gripped with great fear at being left behind. I want you to write this warning to the nations and to the churches because I do not want any left behind. I want you to write and wake up the world and Christians from their millennia of slumber, so that they may ask and receive, that they may hunger and thirst after righteousness, that they may hear me knocking at the door of their heart and open up to receive.

"When they do, my Son, my Holy Spirit and I will come into close relationship and they will receive spiritual power and insight to know and to live lives full of every spiritual blessing, until that day comes— which is fast approaching—when every eye shall see my Son's return—to their joy or to their fear. This is why I have not only gifted you to write, my son, but I have gifted you to hear, so that you may hear me and write my words. And the world and its people may be blessed and be ready for the return of my Son, Jesus Christ."

So it is that I began to write this book, which is not really my book—I am not the author of this book. This is God's book, containing God's words that I typed and recorded on these pages. I also wish to emphasise that I am a sinful man who has done many terribly sinful things of which I am ashamed. I am not a man deserving of God's close attention. I do not understand why God loves me, or why he loves to chat and share with me, but I am sure of this: that if he wants to be a close part of my life, it is certain that he wants to be a very close part of your life too, if you are willing, for you are certain to have lived a better life than I have lived. Nevertheless, God has asked me to write this book and, despite the fact that I know how much trouble it will bring me, I will do what he tells me to do and I will write what he tells me to write, no matter what the consequences will be for me and my life.

The morning of Thursday, February 14, 2013 began like most others. I watched a sermon—this time it was a Jimmy Evans sermon from tfc.org—and afterwards I did some physical exercise. When I went back to my computer to take care of some business, I received clear thoughts from God that I was to begin the process of closing my business and deregistering my company, and I did as I was told.

Soon after this, I felt urged by God to watch a sermon from lifechurch.tv. I asked God, "What sermon?" I got no reply but I felt God wanted me not to just watch any sermon, but a specific one. I opened the website and my eyes were drawn to the #1 link, which was the most recent sermon, and I watched it. It was a sermon named "Altar Ego" by Craig Groeschel. He spoke of being encouraged by a publishing house to write by simply "vomiting up" everything about anything and to send it to the publisher. God's thoughts came into my mind, encouraging me to write in the same way—quickly, without regard to punctuation, grammar or spelling; to simply listen to what God was telling me to write and type as fast as I was able. So that's what I did, and I corrected typos and spelling afterwards.

It was different and strange for me. God's thoughts were in my head with greater clarity. At times, I felt as if I was being taken over by God and that he was using my mind and my body to perform the task of getting his thoughts onto paper. It sometimes felt like I was being used as a channel, with a direct connection between the mind of

God and my fingers. It was a very odd feeling. Sometimes I would become aware that a few hours had passed and that many pages had been typed, but I was not aware of the passage of time. I had no memory of what I had written and, although I felt a little tired in the head, I would rise to put on a coffee. Surprisingly, I would not feel stiff from being in the same position for hours, as I usually did.

I wondered what was happening but I didn't want to ask. Although I knew it was from God, I didn't know what it was and didn't want to spoil it by asking. It was later confirmed to me by God that, on this day, I had been anointed to write for God: This was my calling!

In the sermon by Craig Groeschel that I had been listening to, he also mentioned the difference between what we tell ourselves we are or are not, what others think about us, and what God thinks we are capable of and who he says we really are. These were timely words that God unpacked and personalised for me before I began to write his words for him.

So this is how I came to write these words. The rest is God's story to you, given through me. Whether you believe or do not believe that these are God's words is your decision. I know God hopes, for your sake, that you act on his counsel and that you act fast to put everything you have into following his exhortations.

God anointed me on February 14, 2013 to write his letter to the churches. The Sunday following, the preacher called those who were experiencing the call of God to come forward to be anointed. I knew from God that he had already anointed me but God said it was also important that I receive a public anointing. After I received the anointing with oil from a brother at the front of the church, I looked above me to pray. Soon everything became misty and white. At the top of a tall pillar of cloud that extended about 30 metres, or 100 feet, above me, a white dove fluttered.

As I watched, wondering what was happening, I became immersed with love that felt like it flowed right through me. I felt one with God. Everything then disappeared. I lowered my head and quietly thanked God before returning to my seat. I told no one of my experience, except my wife.

A WORD FROM THE MESSENGER

As you can gather from the title, this section is about me. However, I hope it results in the glory and praise of God and Christ. God has asked me to include this section to assist you.

I must firstly confess to you, that I am a very sinful and weak man. I have committed terrible sins that I dearly wish I hadn't. I struggle to not be immoral, abusive, arrogant, and proud, and I constantly battle against impatience and a bad temper. I am good at being bad and bad at being good. Yet, I also love God, adore his heart, and find peace and security in his arms. As close as I am to my best earthly friend, my wife and soul mate for nearly 40 years, there is no one I treasure in my heart as much as my God, my Christ, my Holy Spirit.

I am not trained in ministry. I am a lay preacher who has occasionally preached and assisted small congregations. I have asked God about getting training but he has always made it clear that he is my teacher and trainer, and he doesn't want me to come under the influence of schools of thought that support various theologies. I have never been important and no one would consider me successful. I have been a happy, invisible nothing and nobody. At times in my life, I have become very busy trying to be a significant somebody but God has intervened to bring me back to earth with a crash, causing me to slow down, so that I would spend time with him. I have found the experience of God slowing me down very frustrating, putting much strain on my impatience—or should that read patience? God has come closer and closer to me and made it abundantly clear, over the decades, that he is seriously and intensely in love with me. Or, to put it to you in a way that I probably shouldn't, God has made it increasingly clear that he is madly and passionately in love with me.

Not that this makes me special, but it does make God very special to me. As I relate to you some details of things that God has done in me and in my life, you may find that my experiences are similar to your own. If you have in your life what I have in mine—God—you are in very good care. If you do not know God, Christ, and the Holy Spirit as I do, I hope this book will help you; and I know the Holy Spirit will help you far more than I can, if you ask him.

Pulling out the "God Card" is frowned on, because it is so easy to abuse, and I can expect that many will frown on this book, thinking that I have pulled out a whole book of "God Cards". I am sorry if you feel this way, and trust me when I say that I am sympathetic to your suspicions. I, however, do not have the luxury of seeing this book in any other way than stated. I would have gladly written a book like others write a book; but this is what I have been given by God to do and, although I can confidently trust that many will howl me down for this, I stand with God, and I can only encourage you to ask for the Holy Spirit's confirmation that this book is what it claims to be.

Am I a prophet? Maybe I am, considering that most prophets in the Bible were sent to call God's children back to obedience. But I am hoping that I am not a prophet of any kind because most were hated and despised by God's disobedient children. I prefer to leave titles and labels for others. I am simply a man told by God to do this, and that is all. I suspect that I am the worst man for the job, but that is God's department. Of this I am certain: that if this book proves to be a blessing to others, the blessing will be all God's doing, and not mine—to his praise, honour and glory.

For about 30 years I was a member of an exclusive church that believes it is the only correct church, and if you go to a different church, you are no longer faithful to Christ, no longer a Christian, no longer saved. God called me out of that exclusive church and into a church that encourages close relationship with God. The way God did this will take longer to describe than I really want to do here. I want to keep my section of the book smaller, because I do not want to risk overshadowing God, who I know is the actual author of this book. Nevertheless, God wants me to share with you, very briefly, some of the experiences I have had with him.

In the first year or so of my Christian walk, I was doing my general nursing training. There were two young men at the hospital who essentially propositioned me along homosexual lines and one committed a mild homosexual assault. About 18 months later, I was chatting with a nursing friend who was still at the hospital, and she told me about the awful deaths of those two young men and how it shocked the staff. Hearing their names, I immediately recalled the unpleasant sexual assault and, just as immediately, I heard words from the Lord in a clear, loud, and angry tone of voice, "I will not allow my little lambs to be touched." I was stunned by what God was implying. Clearly, I did not know my God. I did not know how closely involved he was in my life, and how very personally and seriously he took what others may do to me. I was shaken by what had happened to the two young men.

I was a policeman for six years and, during that time, God gave me a dream that saved my life. The dream from God played out in my sleep, like a short section of a movie, and words came to me, "When you see this happen, when you see this man leave the room, follow him and stay close to him." I also saw a scene in which, as if I had not obeyed these instructions, the man returned to the lounge room with a rifle and shot me and my partner, resulting in one of us being injured and one of us dying. Months later, the footage I had seen in the dream began to play out. I did what God told me to do. Since that day, when I encounter things that make me fearful, God often reminds me that he saved my life that day, that he is the only reason I am alive today, and that I have nothing to fear.

A few years after this, an offender failed to appear in court and I prayed earnestly to God for a few months, asking that he tell me where the offender was. I was in the police station when, suddenly, I saw the name of a small town lit up in my mind as if it were in neon and flashing lights. The words that came to me were: "Phone ---------Police Station, and phone it now!" I thought it was just me—that I had been praying and asking God so often that my mind was now making things up. I didn't phone the police station but I couldn't get it out of my mind and, a few days later, I finally rang the police station, gave the name of the offender, and asked the officer if it meant anything to him. I was shocked when he told me that the offender had been in their watch house, and what a pity I hadn't phoned sooner because they had just released him the day before.

I felt ashamed that I had wasted God's time. I had prayed hard, God had answered, but I had been too stupid to believe and act. I apologised to God that I had not done what he told me to do, and I told God that I understood if he didn't want to waste his time on me again, but if he would give me another chance, I would call straight away. I started praying hard and, not many weeks later, the same thing happened again with the name of a town coming up in neon lights in my mind. It was a different town this time—a few hundred miles from the first. These words came to me: "Phone --------- Police Station, but phone now!" I felt rather stunned and began to hesitate. The words came louder, "BUT PHONE NOW!" I rang the police station and was told that the offender was in a cell in their watch house and that they were about to release him. Due to my diligence and obedience to God's message, they transferred him to my watch house instead so he could appear in court. I went home that afternoon feeling overwhelmed by my God who answers prayer powerfully when it is his will to do so. God's answers made me feel terribly unworthy: God was good to me, but I was a very sinful man. I felt uncomfortably close to God and I asked him to move further away from me; but thankfully he didn't.

About one year later, working with one of the best police partners I ever had the good pleasure of working with, I took a transfer to another police office and, a couple of months later, my former partner was shot and murdered. I felt God's hand in the death of my friend. Years later, I told God that, if I had been there with my friend, I would have done everything possible to save his life, including giving up my own life. God shocked me when he told me that the devil wanted me dead. By sending me the dream that saved my life, a life had to be given to replace mine that was saved, and the life of my friend was the one given so I could live. I sobbed. God explained that there were rules in the unseen realm that I didn't understand. He said he was sorry for my loss, but that it was more important for me to live than my friend because of God's plans for my life.

Then there was the time when I took up roller skating with my 14-year-old daughter so that I could keep the young guys away from her—a "must do" for all dads. God began sending me visions in the day and in the night, and he was also giving me dreams at night. All the visions and dreams were about someone taking a bad fall at the skating rink and receiving a painful injury. Within a few weeks, God made it clear that I was the one who would be injured. The visions and dreams showed me the day, the time, and even the particular song that would be playing at the time of my fall.

I ignored all the warnings, preferring to believe it must be my imagination rather than believing it was from God. I thought I would prove that it was only coming from me by skating right through the song unscathed. However, I did fall and smashed the bones in my arm into 18 fragments. I needed a bone graft and a metal rod to repair the damage. As a result, I now have a wrist that is solid and cannot move. It is a constant reminder for me to listen to my God, who can spare me suffering. With the gift of 20/20 hindsight, I felt like a fool. But God was very kind, reminding me that I would never have known how real the warnings were, had I not been on the rink and had no one been hurt. Pain is a great teacher!

Quite recently, God again saved my life and the life of my family too! Halfway through last year, my wife, my daughter, my granddaughter and I were driving north of Brisbane to enjoy a beautiful day at the beach. Along the way, I noticed a small car with a young woman passenger and a young man driving. The young man had his arm out the window and generally looked like he was about as attentive as if he were sitting on his sofa at home. He and his girlfriend were always looking down at something, probably Facebook. We drove past them and, on the way, the road narrowed to just one lane and the speed limit dropped to 80 kilometres per hour. Then the traffic slowed to a complete stop. About a hundred metres behind us, I could see that same small car with the young couple, and it was still travelling at 80 kilometres or more, with the driver completely oblivious to our stopped car and all the other stopped cars.

I was looking in the rear vision mirror so I was the only one in our car who knew what was happening. Without God doing something, I expected we would all die in the next few seconds. I quickly and simply committed all of us into God's care and left it in his hands. When the small sedan was only 5 or 6 metres (about 20 feet) from slamming straight into the back of our car and killing us all, I witnessed the miracle of the small car, with no ABS and all wheels fully locked up, and with no steering, being pushed sideways by a force that sent it clear of the back of our car, turned it 180 degrees, and made it slide backwards up an embankment about 200 metres (650 feet) from our car.

I was so thankful to God for saving my family, and I told God that I knew I had just seen something impossible. God simply confirmed for me that the powerful angels, who protect me and my family, had simply done their job. My little granddaughter was asleep, and my wife and daughter noticed the noise, and the car flashing past us and leaving the road backwards. I described the miracle I had witnessed and encouraged them to thank God for saving their lives. Having attended and investigated many collisions as a police officer, I have a lot of experience and knowledge of what vehicles can and cannot do. And all the laws of physics made it impossible for that car to do anything but hurtle into us. God broke the laws of physics to protect us.

While all these things were happening with God, there was an uncomfortable collision of beliefs between my church, on one side, believing that God doesn't do anything powerful anymore and God, on the other side, who was doing a lot of powerful things in my life. To avoid upsetting people, I mostly kept secret what God was doing. As I disregarded my church's opinions, God was still very active in my life, and I wondered if my experiences were normal.

I related a few of the incidents in an email to a preacher friend, in Los Angeles, and asked him if he knew what was happening. He told me it was God and said that I was receiving a powerful calling; that whatever it was, it was big and it would be dangerous for me to say "no" to God. It was a long and frustrating wait—not knowing the nature of my calling and when I would be called. Each life change that came along would have me wondering if this was the calling that God had in mind for my life. I lived wondering about my calling until early in 2013.

Back to my recount of events: More years passed and I was with a church where members were distressed by plans to sell the building and relocate the congregation to another area. I began to feel powerfully prompted by God to inform the preacher that I could not agree to the sale of the church property since it caused distress to members (at that time, I was one of the trustees and had my name on the Deed of Title). God pestered my thoughts night and day, and did not let me rest until I agreed to block the preacher's plans.

However, if I stopped the church sale, I would be shunned by the people and lose friendships that had existed for decades. Before I agreed, and even though I knew that God knew everything and that he knew what he was doing, I asked him if he knew what he was asking me to do—that my name would be dragged through the mud, and that I would be shunned if I did what he was asking me to do. God confirmed that he knew what he was asking me to do; he knew people would despise me, but he wanted me to do it for him. So I did it. I met with the preacher and, at the end of our meeting, he reminded me that I had a very good name in the church, a name so good that many people would love to have the good name and reputation I had. He advised that I not do this to myself and told me that, if I were to immediately desist, he would never tell anyone that the conversation with me had ever taken place. I assured the preacher that it was God and not me—that I had no choice—that God would not let me rest or sleep until I did it. So it was that I did it for the Lord; I lost my good name and was shunned by most. Nevertheless, my relationship with God grew closer.

One night, a couple of years after this, I was visited by two angels. I was terrified until one of the angels touched me, and instantly my fear was replace by a euphoric feeling of peace, love, and safety. I asked the Lord why the angels had visited me, and the Lord asked me how I felt. I told him that I felt loved and close to him. The Lord confirmed that this was why the angels had visited.

About 10 years ago, God wanted me to confess shocking secret sins to my wife. I told God that I couldn't confess them to my wife unless he was there with me. God assured me that he would be there with me. I told God that, if I could not see him, I could not do what he was asking. God appeared in the Spirit and he remained with me to strengthen me. I told God that if, due to my confessions to my wife, she would hate me and divorce me, I would never love him again, I would never talk to him again, and I would never want to see him again. My amazingly kind and loving wife forgave me! Many times I have deeply regretted those terribly hurtful words that I said to my God, and every time I raise it with him, and feel distressed over hurting him, his gentle and understanding reply is always words to the effect of, "David, you were distressed; it is okay!" How wonderfully loving and kind is our God. The treasure of all treasures is the heart of our God and Christ.

About five years ago, during a time of prayer, Scripture reading, and meditation in the Spirit, I was surprised to see God, Christ, and the Holy Spirit standing in my lounge room. They looked like they were discussing something together. Then Christ turned to me and, before they disappeared, he said, "The decision has been made to bless you!" I wondered what form that blessing would take.

Approximately a year after that, I was chatting with the Lord and I asked him why my calling was taking so long to be revealed. The Lord told me that it wasn't a case of me waiting for them, but they were waiting for me. I was not ready. God said that the task would destroy me through pride if it came too early. I was told to focus my efforts on coming closer and closer to the Father, the Son, and the Holy Spirit in my relationship. I asked the Lord how big my calling was and I saw a vision of the whole planet. Words came to me that my calling would bless the church, and the kingdom worldwide, and that it would initiate a great revival. I believed the Lord, even though I could not imagine how that could possibly happen.

It was not long after this, when I was sharing time with the Lord and, knowing that rabbis customarily changed the names of their followers, I asked God if there is a new name that he would like to give me. One word came back to me: "Emmanuel." I was shocked and thought this could not be coming from God, for only the Christ could use the name that means "God with us." God explained that I didn't understand something very basic, and that this is why I was concerned to receive the name "Emmanuel". He explained that the thoughts in my head, the feelings in my heart, and the words in my mouth should be his thoughts, feelings, and words. He went on to say that I should have the mind of Christ, that all Christians—myself included—should be "Emmanuel" to the world; and if we are not, then we are not in Christ. We are not disciples of Christ.

A short time later, I was in worship and praising God when, suddenly, in a vision, there was a dark face about three inches in front of my face, staring into my eyes. It was my Lord and he said, "David, come close, and I will explode out of you."

On another occasion during worship, I saw the vision of a man speaking to an enormous number of people, and he spoke with powerful confidence. It looked like me but what I was doing was more than I could do. As I watched this man speak, the Lord said, "That is you with me inside you."

'The Valentine Prophecies' is my calling, and my impatient waiting now over. Thank you, Lord. At last, this is my calling.

THE

VALENTINE

PROPHECIES

Please Note: I have largely suspended quotation marks
as these are mostly God's words.

A CALL TO WRITE

Thursday, February 14, 2013

David, I call you to my side today to be my servant and to write what I tell you to write. I know you will do that, for this is what I have prepared you for, and every day before today has led you to this day, to begin the task for which you were born. You will not feel much like it is your task for this is my book, my writing, my words, and you are my scribe. Yet you are important to my purpose for I have trained you to hear my words. I have moved close into your heart and mind. And you have the strength and courage to give this to the world, in my name, and receive the mocking and wrath of this world, and their scorn, for they will not believe you. But I send this book into all the world anyway because of my love for them. Fill up your mind and your heart with my spirit, David, so that you may have the mind of Christ and write faithfully and true.

To those who believe, and listen, and do, more will be given and they will be blessed.

David, tell them I am coming quickly. I am coming soon. Many are asleep, many are in sin, many are arguing and fighting over my Scriptures and they have forgotten me.

WHAT HAS HAPPENED TO THE CHURCH?

I am deeply grieved by the churches, let alone the world. I sorrow for both the church and the world. While churches argue together, the world hurts and receives no clear message, no clear example—only the rumble of dissention and strife. Is this my voice to the world? Am I the God of confusion? I hate what has happened to my church. I hate what has happened to my truth. It has been torn apart by scholars like a surgeon dissects a cadaver, as if by their search of the microscopic they can find life. Instead they kill the life from my Word and are left with words without power.

How can I minister through academics? Was my Son an academic? My Son loved me and knew me, listened to me, knew my voice, and did what I told him. Tell the churches they will do well to do likewise.

I apologise to the world for the church has been so faithless. Where are the leaders who listen to me? Where are the men who will go to the lost and lead them back to me? How can you lead to a place you do not know?

The church is like a business. It is a corporation. Books must balance; lights and new carpets are important—more important than my truth, more important than loving me and being true to me.

When I lie down, I sorrow. Too many, David, too many will cry out on the last day saying, "I never knew—they were always fighting—I tried church but they hated me—I wanted to know you God, but they didn't know you."

3

David, my church—the price paid to redeem it—the sacrifice of my Son, has it been in vain? I have warned for thousands of your years that the end will come. It will surprise many: one will be taken, another left. Will any be taken?

I sorrow for those left—what are they left to, David? Do you care? Does anyone on earth care? I am a mournful God. These are the last days, and I should have a cheerful message, a message brimming with satisfaction, overflowing with contentment. But how can I, for who has listened to my words?

Mush, mush, and more mush; this is what I hear. Everyone wants to hear mush. Everyone wants to preach mush. My servants, the preachers, preach mush. Where is the hope for anything good to come out of service from servants who do not know me, who do not know my Word, who do not know what I value?

I want hearts, David—not mush. I long after close relationship with man, now and forevermore—always have, always will. Will you write this? Will you tell them? Will they receive it? Will they listen?

Many in high and mighty spiritual positions will mock my words through you, my servant David. They are self-appointed to positions that I never gave them. They sit alone.

The church has become a trap to many—a trap so many cannot escape from—they are trapped in the business of doing church, of programmes and running the business, of stepping up the ladder of success. This is my church for Pete's sake. What on earth do they think they are doing? They have lost their way and there seems to be no way back.

But David, there really is a way back. They will be given a way back—a far more difficult and costly way back.

For I know they do not do what they really want to do. They are not really those kinds of people: Inwardly they adore me—inside they want me—but the clutter of church stuff and church things makes them a servant to stuff and things, and not a servant of the Most High.

AN UNBELIEVABLE MESSAGE

As it was in the days of Noah, they took him for a fool, a speaker of falseness, a man of foolishness, a liar, a deceiver. As unbelievable as my message was through Noah, so it is through you, David.

After Noah took his last step from the earth beneath his feet, from the world about to be doomed to destruction, he left behind him the scoffers and was lifted to redemption with those who listened—his family. So it is with you David, they will dash your words to the ground and hate and despise you. But on a day fast approaching—not far off now—it will be as it is written—as it was spoken from the mouths of my faithful prophets. There will be those who join their Bridegroom in the sky and there will be those left behind.

Those who, deep down, have a heart for me but have not become one with me now, in this life, will be left. Many who thought church was a means to wealth or prominence will then know it is not. Many who think church is enough and attend, leaving their heart outside, will then know it is not.

David, it will soon be terrifying for those left to the unrestrained hatred of the one to come. He is already here. He is awaiting his moment. As Christ is receiving his glory, so will the evil one rise up to grasp and clutch for glory—a glory that rides on a sea of blood—the blood of martyrs who know they were not taken. Then they will examine the Scriptures. Then they will cry out. Then they will give anything to be saved for they shall believe and want to save themselves from hell.

Please, David, tell them I want to spare them. I don't want any to go through what comes swiftly. The earth will become a living hell.

Many lamps are without oil. They are not waiting for me; they are having fun. They have created their own redemption. They have lost their way. My Son is the Way; no one comes to the Father except by him. This is not just a message for the sincere Islamist and for the devoted Jew. And this is not just a message for worshippers of idols or for those who are cynics of anything spiritual. This is also a message for Christians. What does my Son mean when he says, "I am the Way"? What happens to the Way if the church gets in the way?

LEFT BEHIND

David, we must clear the small path to eternal life. It is not big, but it is straight and clear. But the churches have placed thistles and briars to snag as many as venture along it in their desire to reach me. They snag them for their churches. They convert them to their system, their method, their way! Enough! We are near the end of the way. We are at the gates. It is time. Everything is ripe. Everything is ready. The table is set, the food is out, the aroma of delicious food is steaming and streaming out through the doors of heaven; there is no way to keep in what is so good.

Does the church smell the scent of heaven? No! Why not, David? Because it is too busy. They will weep and mourn over their programmes, their rites, their divisions.

They will have no programmes, no rites, and no divisions when the wicked are unleashed against them. There will only be one believer then, only one church, only one belief, only one way. That will be the way of martyrdom. There will be unity then. None of the believers will ask, "Where do you worship? What church do you attend? What do you believe?" For all will be one—united in Christ.

David, don't you get it? Those who are left behind will stand on legs without power. They will stand in the strength they have. It will be enough because of love—because of their love for me and because of my love for them—it will be enough. They will find the way. They will fall in love with me, they will know me as friend, they will hear my voice, be saved, and I will bring them home. But they do not have to go through hell to get to heaven.

This is why I speak now, I warn now. There is an easier way. They can prepare now with hearts that hear and be lifted up when I call them to join me in the clouds. The difference between the celebration in the skies that will occur on that day, David, and the terror that will grip the believers who are left behind, is greater than words. I hate to think of anyone feeling as they will. I want them all with me.

Please warn them; please get this out to them quickly. I am coming quickly. The end nears! The signs are in place—everything is ripe.

WHY NAME THE CHURCHES?

Friday, February 15, 2013

David, why the different names? I'll tell you why. When you name something, you own it—it is yours. I brought the animals to my son Adam to name. I was giving them to him. I gave him ownership over them and a symbol of his ownership was that he named them. When people have children, they name them, they belong to them, and their children are theirs. David, when did I ever give my church to my children to name? When did I give up my church? When did I give it away?

So now, we have all these names and they all represent me differently. And when they do that, are they not all tainted? Are they not all statements that testify to the fact that they do not trust me, that they do not have faith in me? They are testimony to the fact that my children are saying I do not have the power to own and to run a successful church. Then why is it that I seem perfectly capable of having made the church explode in numbers in the first century?

When did my children decide to begin insulting me, their Father and Most High God? When did I become, in their eyes, not enough, not up to the task? When did I become second rate compared to what proud man can do? David, as it was in Nazareth, my children who know me best, who are most familiar with me, who are closest to me, are the very ones who think they know me well enough to say that I cannot do "that" anymore. Was it I who stopped doing, or was it they who stopped believing?

David, my son, today there are some who say they are miracle workers. But their works are lies, their miracles are lies. They are deceivers. And why? To get a name, to get wealth, to become famous, and to have a following of fans. And where do I fit into that? Where do my Son, my Holy Spirit and I enter into that? These are ministries of deceit and we know the deceiver.

There are some whose very theology, whose beliefs, put a ban on my power. Their missionaries in the third world are casting out demons and healing by my power, but when they return home to report on their work, they do not report on my work—what my power has done—and they deny me the praise and the glory that is rightfully mine. These are perverted gospels, words without power. Many sincere people are troubled by their lies, lies they are forced to say so they can maintain the party line, be seen as good Christians, as faithful. Faithful to what? Not faithful to their God, but faithful to a church that is indoctrinated with untruths—untruths about me. Since when does my church spread untruths about me? The leaders of these churches do not know me and will not let any of their converts know me. They are puffed up. Their churches are puffed up. If a man can recite the whole of my Holy Word by memory, what good is it to him, if he does not know me? I am the reason for the church. I love. I have a plan. I have a way. Everything I want for people is love; it is only good. Why must they add?

Many say, "But what have we added? The other churches have added. Not us. We have it perfect. We are the perfect church. We are the only church that has it right. You have to get it right to please God and go to heaven. And if you go elsewhere, if you go to another church, you have it wrong and you will go to hell." As they condemn others, they condemn themselves with hollow doctrines, hollow lives. When did they ask me? When did I tell them this? Did they conclude this on their own? Yes, I tell you, they concluded this lie on their own, and they stand alone on their lies. Do not be amongst them.

Why am I saying all this, David? Why am I talking harshly to my sons and daughters? This is not the voice I use when I talk to you, David. I am gentle with you, but now you hear me angry and hurt. You feel my grief and sorrow. Think about it and understand.

If I cannot wake these who are tainted—these who are half born—if I cannot cause them to listen now, what then? The Bridegroom comes. He is approaching now. Don't you feel him, David? I know that you do. You know power is being poured out from my Spirit upon the earth to awaken all who have a heart for me—all who have a minute amount of hope in their hearts. Jesus rightly says he does not know the hour but, David, if you can see the signs and feel the heightening power and rushing of the Spirit, does not Jesus, my Son, feel it too? This is why he is now approaching the door of the great feast. The tables are being prepared. My servants are busy and the excitement is rising. Everyone is preparing and excited in heaven, David. Where is the excitement on earth? It is devoted to doing stuff and things. You must wake them up to lift their eyes above what they have made—above their self-made churches—to me, to their Christ.

RELATIONSHIP WITH GOD

If they fail to listen, what then? David, how much more do I long for my children to repent now and rush into relationship with me, with hearts wide open, than to ignore me by ignoring you. Then they shall be left and not be caught into the clouds of heaven. Then they shall repent with fear and trembling. I am troubled. My heart lays bare. I bare my open heart to you. Feel my grief. I ache, David, for those who will repent after the Saints are removed. How much happier all my children and all people of the earth, who have a longing for me and my love and my heart, would be to rise, with my Son, in the clouds of heaven, to be taken into my arms. There will be great joy—greater joy than there has ever been. What a glorious day in heaven. I want all my children with me on that day. I don't want it to be a case of repentance driven by terror. I want them to repent now—to bring their hearts to me now, in peace. That is what I want.

David, do you recall when my Son was asked, when he was tested by one of the teachers, what's it really all about? What's the most important thing? What does it all come down to? My Son told him, and others there, love the Lord your God with all your heart, soul, mind and strength, and love your neighbour as yourself. David, nothing has changed. Love the heart of your God with everything you have; love your neighbour and yourself.

David, like today, Jesus was speaking to people who had forgotten. Yes they had religion, devotions, Scripture, giving, fine buildings, budgets, but they might as well have been worshipping an image—a dead image. They had no relationship with the living God. The accounts of my love for my people and the great things I had done were things in a book. These things were not in their hearts. They were not taking them personally. They didn't really believe them. That is why they were not living them. They were not living as if there were a God who was living.

David, do you know how much I ache for the hearts of my children? Why did I make the universe? Do I need it? Did I need something to do? I made people with a heart like mine—people who could love. All people have come out of me. I have made myself vulnerable because of my love. Every person I ever created is my child. They are all mine. It hurts when my children hate and despise me. It also hurts when my children assemble every Sunday to praise me with their lips but their hearts are far from me. Their minds are on how much money was collected. Will it meet budget? Or was the praise in tune? Or was it warm enough, cool enough, comfortable enough? Or did the kids enjoy it, and the old people, and did women enjoy it? Did everyone approve? Will they be back next week? Will more hear how great it is and bring their friends? And then there will be more and more, and bigger and bigger of the same. But is that better?

Where do I fit into that, David? Where do I belong in all of that? I do not belong at all. I do not fit in at all. I am a seeker of hearts. These people are seekers of fun and pleasure—instant pleasure. They go elsewhere—maybe to the beach. If these people truly knew me, they would know that I am fun, I am pleasure, I am a delight. They would know how much I long for them to know the real me and be complete and completely satisfied by me. My first children, Adam and Eve, were not content. The moment Satan suggested there was more and something better, they wanted it. The truth is, David, that Satan is a liar, and there is nothing better than being in me.

DIVIDED HEARTS

David, do you remember when that angel touched you? "Yes Lord," I replied. What did you feel David? "I felt a total and complete elation, tranquillity, liberty, and a sense of safety—it was a euphoric rush like I have never known before or since." What you were feeling was my heart. That is heaven. That is eternity. That is me. That is what my angels live with and feel all the time. It is good. I give what is good. I give what is the very best. People must let go of what they have in order to receive, from me, what they do not have. What I have for them is what they are desperately needing, wanting, and aching for. But they must lay aside what they love now to receive from me.

Their divided heart hurts me. I will not be treated like trash, David. You know that. I am not garbage but, when people come to me with a divided heart, they receive so little, they want so little, and they blame me for giving them so little. There is no room in their hearts for anything else. They have their first love. They have already chosen. I ask them to choose again, while they can, with my power to help them.

Churches have filled their own ears with their own praise, their own worship, to their own glory. I am not enough for them, and no wonder, David, for they do not know me. In this modern age, education, technology, medicine, construction, and all the new conveniences capture the hearts of my people. There is no room in the hearts of the people for me. I am not exciting enough—not as exciting as the latest iPhone, camera, computer tablet, wristwatch, kitchen, bathroom, shoes, jewellery, make-up, dresses, suits, hair styles, cars, motorcycles, boats, houses. Let's not mention qualifications that make one person feel so much smarter and more capable than another.

Incomes divide. The rich sneer at the poor and the poor call the rich snobs.

Who, by qualification, will pass through the gates of heaven? Who, by riches and possessions, will buy their way in? And who, by beauty and flattery, will open that door? Puffed up fools, David; snares of the devil.

David, people would rather miss heaven, than miss a TV show. So much time is lost to TV, Facebook, and electronic devices. Their God, their first love, is their TV and Facebook. There is no time to waste. If they want a relationship with me, I am not hard to find. Am I hiding? Do they call out and I run and hide? I am here, David. I am the corner shop they walk past every day, saying, "I must drop in there someday". Am I not where their friends are? I am not cool? I am not popular? So they swap friendship with me for friendship with their friends. Did their friends make heaven? Have I cheapened myself? Am I too accessible? Am I too available? Am I not always there, always here, always right beside each one of them? And is that why time with me is despised?

After my children are caught up into the clouds of heaven, those left behind, those who went to church, and those who thought they should go to church but the shops were open and it was more fun to go shopping, and those who wanted to play sports or go to the beach will weep, knowing they were left behind. Then the Bibles will come out; then churches will fill; then TVs and Facebook will be turned off. And people will cry out to me, will seek my counsel and will desire to follow me more than anyone or anything else. Why not today? They can make the change today, if they believe.

WHO WILL BE LEFT BEHIND?

What is something that grieves me, David? "Yesterday, Lord, you described to me the anguish of parents whose little children will be caught up into the clouds of heaven—the separation, the horror of being left to an evil world which will then be filled with hate, without redeeming love or hope. Families will be split along the spiritual divide—marriages too." Then they will know I was serious—as in the days of Noah—and then they will not mock our words. I ask them to prick up their ears, to lift their eyes, for soon I will send my Son. The hour is near. They have been told.

Will there be many preachers caught up to Christ? No, there will not be many preachers. They will not listen now but they will listen then. Many will be surprised to see preachers left behind but they, and most others, will then have a new heart, will search the Scriptures, will listen, believe, and do as I say. They will then have a heart for me and, though the earth will descend into a hellish state, they will rise up and stand for me, and they will be the first of multitudes to die for my name and the name of my Son. Why not today? My plea is for a new spirit, a new heart—repentance today.

THE TRUTH ABOUT RELATIONSHIPS

Arrogance, it is arrogance when anyone adds to or takes from my Holy Word. Yet all have done it; all are doing it. It began in the first century. Men thought they would water down Christ because preaching him brought on trouble. It was more popular to wink at the local pagan philosophies. Christ was painted in all sorts of ways, other than true. Women thought they would dominate by their volume and many words. But I had good men in the first century who knew the truth, corrected error, and their corrections were endorsed by my power.

So it is today, that there is error. They are teaching to appeal to the world or to gratify their egos. Error has always been easier than truth. The biggest difference today is that there are not as many men who are standing up and correcting as there were in the first century.

David, you know I love you dearly, but I have given you a tough assignment in a tough age. As it was with my Son, he was not qualified. He was a nobody from nowhere who had done nothing impressive. Those who should have known better, the Pharisees, found such offence in him that, even the mighty and righteous things he did in my name, and by my power, were appropriated to the devil. You know you are an evil man who has committed evil offences; you are a nothing and a nobody. People will not believe you and, instead, will despise you.

Nevertheless, there will be some who listen to my Holy Spirit, who understand that what you are saying is truth and is from me. To those who have the mind of Christ, who can hear the voice calling them to repentance and to transformation, to them I write these words: Pray and fast. Go to a quiet place. Get the clamber of life out of your ears. Sit with me humbly. Don't instruct me. Ask me to lead you from where you are to where you should be. When I share with you, you must listen and do what I say.

Rubbish of man has been mixed with my truth. Remove this contamination for it makes the believers sick. Nourishment and strength come from the truth; weakness and frailty come from falsehood. Turn back to the Scriptures, open my Book, and read and listen to me. Stop telling me what I mean. Stop telling me I am out of date, and that no morals are the morals of today, and that you must appeal to the people with no morals to get the big numbers and the success you crave. I gave the church moral teaching. Teach it!

I taught men to be men but even men laugh at men today and call them mice—and men stand for it. Even women think they are bigger, better, smarter and faster than men. I want to remind women that the first to sin was the woman. She was my little girl for whom I had done everything, and she tossed me aside for her ego. She thought she made a better god than me. Women, be careful where you stand. You are full of self-congratulations. But when I look at you, all I can see is shame and loss. Who you are cannot be covered up. Your many words are not for boasting, but are foolishness. Have I not already told you that wisdom is found in few words and foolishness in your excitable self-glorifying chatter?

Men, why have you laid yourselves at the feet of women as if you are their slaves, as if they must be worshipped? It is fools who adore fools. Stand up and be the men I made you to be, and lead your women, your children, your churches to righteousness. It was you I made first and in you I was completely satisfied. You and I chatted and shared. It was you who needed a woman, not me. I made the woman for the man. I made men to lead, to protect, to provide, and to love your women and your children. Wherever women push you, you go. They push you away from your children and call you inferior to them. They push you out of the workplace and call you inferior to them. They push you out of the churches and call you inferior to them.

Men and women, hear me when I speak. Men, when you do not love and lead your wife, you dishonour me. Women, as much as you dishonour your husband, you dishonour me. You are both made in my image. You are both equally amazing creations—works of art. Women, stop walking all over men. Men, get up and stop being walked over. Men, do not submit to your wife. Does Christ submit to the church? Yes, right now the churches think so. I am not the God of confusion. Men, rule over your wife and children as Christ rules over the church. Women, submit to your husband as the church must submit to Christ.

It grieves me to see such sorrows in your homes, in your relationships, in your churches. As you are loved by me and by my Son, so you must love each other. It is not for you to claim to be better or best. As I have made you, so you are. Did any of you make yourself a man? Did any of you make yourself a woman? So if you are not self-made, then how dare you criticise how I have made a man or how I have made a woman? Have I made garbage? Are the created to question the Creator? What level of self-deluded arrogance is this? Fools, fools, you watch your TVs and model yourselves on miserable, corrupted, contemptible lives. You model yourselves on idolaters; and are you not idolaters when you despise the people I have made. Who made you people my judge? The best you can do is love each other with the love with which I have loved you. I have told you. Now get away from your TVs and your mirrors filled with selfish, gloating and inflated egos, and humble yourselves to me and to each other, for when I look at you men and you women, all I see is people who have failed me and failed each other. Climb down from your loftiness, prostrate yourselves before me and before each other and, from that humble position, begin to love me and begin to love each other. For you were made for love, humble love, and not for gloating, boasting, pride, and ridicule of others.

I feel weighed down with sorrow and I cannot share words to describe how I feel. I love you my children. Even though you despise me, defy me, will not listen, and will not come near to be blessed, I love you. Love rushes up and overwhelms me whenever I think of you. I despair at your sorrows. You are so far from me.

How can I even say, please come back to me, when you have never been close? You will be—oh, you will be—when you have to fight for it, when it is taken away from you, when you are denied the right to speak my name without bleeding for it. Oh, you will know spiritual hunger and thirst like you have never known it. You will rush after me. You will cling to me; we will be close. And I will be your Father and you will be my children. Please, it is so much easier for you to fall into my open arms today. Hear my voice today, I plead. Have I been too harsh? Maybe, maybe not. To some, I may appear to be too harsh for this letter is not to everyone.

There are some—and you know who you are—in the east and west, who adore me. You search my heart. You plunge deeply into my love. You dive into my Holy Word to be sure of what pleases me, because you want to express your love in more than words and feelings. Some know persecution now. You know whose you are and in the clouds of heaven you shall be with the Christ. Oh, what a day of rejoicing that will be.

You know the meaning of my words when I told, long ago, that I desire a contrite heart above sacrifices. People who truly know who they are and what they deserve for their sins, are humble and thankful, and what is in their hearts fills my heart to overflowing with good pleasure. Such people know they are naked, unloved nothings, except for Christ.

WHAT IS GOD OFFERING?

Will Satan clothe you? Will he love you? Will he lift you up to be honoured and adored? Do not share in Satan's future.

I offer you to share the future with me. Where I am and what I have made for you is beyond words. In this life, you receive my love, my power, my salvation. I come to share with you even my eternal life. You will become beneficiaries of life eternal. I have held little back. You cannot imagine what I have given to thrill you. I created the whole universe so that you would all someday step into my paradise and share my house and all my good things. My heart is the most generous heart you will ever experience. I am sweet and gentle. You will not be disappointed, far from it, you will be overwhelmed. Please give me your whole heart today. Don't look back. Don't look around you. Don't be distracted. Make me yours today and let's together step into the most wonderful eternity in my paradise. It is easier for those who have nothing and no one to value me and what I have for them.

WHAT IS GOD TEACHING?

Be wary of your teachers and your churches. I am the only one you can trust. Sit quietly, somewhere private; open my Holy Word and start reading. When you are working, if you can have your computer reading my Scriptures to you, do that. Keep asking me to help you to understand. Ask me where you should attend church. Be prepared to hear from me, and when you do, do as I say, because I am here to help, to bless, to love and to lead you home to my home.

On Baptism

About baptism: What do I say? I say it washes you of your sins. I say it is when you are reborn and become my spiritual babe. This is not John's baptism. This is not simply baptism of repentance. This is baptism in the name of Jesus, in the name of Christ, in the name of Father, Son, and Holy Spirit. Or in other words, this is baptism into your God. When a person turns to me, believing and desiring in their heart to listen to me and follow me, baptise them as soon as practicable. If you are not near water, take them to water deep enough to plunge them under. Baptise them into Christ, and they will be added to his church and will rise to a new spiritual life in Christ, a new life in me, a new life in the Holy Spirit.

Is baptism an urgent thing to do or can you wait for next Sunday, next year, next summer, your next lifetime? Well, is being cleansed of your sins of interest to you foolish people?

Why are you delaying baptism for sometimes years or decades? And many never get baptised because they cannot see the point. I sympathise with them not seeing the point because you have taken away the point of baptism. I sympathise with you in your delusion about baptism because you have grown up in this and many other errors, and you cannot see or know the truth clearly due to all the different "truths" around. Listen to the Holy Spirit for he will teach you correctly; and the truth will set you free of your disunity and confusion, and place you on solid ground.

On Trusting

Stop telling me I am wrong. What do you do from the very beginning? You teach my babes that I have it wrong—that the church and the church teachers have it right. But oh, whatever you do, don't trust me, don't trust God. You cannot lead and not trust God. You cannot save and not trust God. You cannot be saved and not trust God. Stop being my enemy. Stop being the friend of Satan. Get your empty, condemning words out of the hearts and heads of my little ones. I am serious when I say, "take me seriously and take my Holy Word seriously."

Today, after many centuries of compromising my Holy Word, your consciences have been seared. "Everyone is doing it; it has to be okay," you think. Can it be so wrong? A little nip here, a little tuck there? Do you not understand that my Holy Word is like a holy garment to you? You make alterations and it no longer fits; it no longer serves its purpose; it no longer protects from the hostile spiritual environment that it must protect you from.

I know that many of you are acting unwittingly. I understand that and I have been patient for centuries. Christ's blood, my Son's sacrifice, is powerful, but I want everyone to now take account of themselves as a teacher, as to what you are teaching. If it is not in my Holy Scriptures, don't teach it. If it is in my Holy Scriptures, teach it. Why is everyone so deceived into thinking this is difficult? Who has put that into your heads? Not me! Listen to me. Get back to Scripture. Honour your God and honour your Christ by getting back to the truth of the Holy Scriptures. Some of you have people signing documents and parade these processes as things spiritual. This is rubbish. Are those documents from heaven? Did I print them? Stop it!

On Truth

What does my Holy Word say? Did I not tell you to ask if you wanted wisdom? Why don't you ask? You went to some seminary, got a bit of paper, and were indoctrinated and contaminated with a form of truth that is twisted and far from the truth that I gave you.

Do you think this is a game? Can we all sit around and throw ideas into a big circle and pick out what we want and leave what we don't want? Don't you realise there is a war going on? Satan wants you all dead. Satan is powerful. If you live for more than a moment, it is by my powerful protection. My Holy Word is a frontline defence to you all. Stop watering it down and poking it full of holes and making Satan's job all the easier and my job all the more difficult.

Teachers, listen to me. I have heard it said that Jesus never drank alcohol, that it is sin to drink alcohol, but what do I say? What does Jesus say? Teachers, listen to me. I have heard that you learn and train, and that you are ordained after you agree to a certain set of teachings of beliefs that are peculiar to a particular church or group of churches? What are you saying… that there are different truths? Am I divided? Is there a different Holy Word in your different churches? This is blasphemy and I am indignant. Teachers, humble yourselves before me. If it helps you, put on sackcloth and ashes. If it helps you, fast. I warn you now that, if you do not repent, I will refine your hearts like gold through a fire. You will tremble, you will shake, you will quake in terror and remember these words of warning as you note and come to the realisation that you have missed the clouds of heaven. Be warned, the Words of my Son are life, but you are killing them.

On The Holy Word

You put at risk my little ones, for the sake of your traditions. You must not upset the establishment or tarnish your good name. No, instead you trample my Holy Word as if it were sport, like a football to kick around for your fun. My word is treasure of such high value that you can never buy it, yet for the pay of your wages and the respect you receive for walking in your churches, feeling like big shots, you savage it like wild pigs, tearing into it and devouring it like a pig eats garbage. My Holy Word is everything but garbage and you will respect it now, or you will respect it after you are refined by the very events written in its prophecies.

Approach my Holy Word, as you should your salvation, with fear and trembling. What have my teachers become…spiritual barbarians—beasts of the field—mere animals without understanding? You will understand, but I plead with you as a Father to his children, that you listen to the wisdom of your Father today, while peace and comfort remain at your doorstep. Please listen to me, my children, for I love you and I adore you.

On Sin

I have heard that homosexuals are in the ministry, held up as honourable and as mentors, as holy lives to imitate. Am I now forced to follow the churches in their moral failures and tarnish my holiness and purity, and dignify your filth? Have you not read that your best attempts at a most holy life are filth compared to what my Son, my Holy Spirit and I call righteousness? To not be content with the filth of your righteousness and to slip gloatingly, brashly, proudly into a mire of dishonour, is like…I cannot find words to describe how far you are from me.

I love homosexuals; they are my children. Their sin is no worse than lusting over pornography, adultery, or any other immorality, but you want to call it a non-sin now. When did you ever become the judge of what is holy and what is not holy? When did you ever qualify to set standards? This is my Holy Word. These are my holy standards. How dare you condemn others to never rise above your own filth, to never rise above your own sins, to never rise to liberty in Christ, but to stand condemned in their own sins that you condoned? And you authorised sin by your own authority. What authority?

Who made you God? What do you know about sin? What do you know about the massive price my Son paid for your filth? I am sobbing now. Do you know how much I love my Son? Do you know what it took for me to turn and withdraw my love, withdraw myself, withdraw my presence from my Son at his darkest hour? It tore me apart. When he cried out, don't you think I heard? It destroyed me. A part of me died with my Son—we had never been apart. I hated moving away— far away—but I had to, or I would not be God. Words do not describe how much your filth must be kept far from me. We are serious about love. We are serious about sin. Love is life. Sin is death. If you want to be with me forever, accept my Son's blood covering, humbly remove your filth, and never call your sin righteousness. To know what is righteous, you must be righteous. And you, who teach that you can practice sin and make it the holiness of God, are gravely deceived. You are hell-bound unless you fill up on our Spirit, his wisdom, and receive the mind of Christ. But right now, you have the mind of Satan and are his servants.

Women excuse their gossip, calling it harmless, saying they are just being women. Gossip is hate. I made you to love. Stop excusing what makes me vomit. Women are always right; children know everything. What is wrong with you people? You disgust me. Gluttony is looked upon as okay. Show me where I ever said that. Women, dress modestly and stop wearing tight, revealing clothing and judging men as disgusting when they look. And men, stop excusing your weaknesses in your sex-drive and take control. Everyone today has an excuse for everything. Your marriages fail. Women blame men, men blame women, and your children are the victims of your hate and your lack of responsibility. Men and women, stop picking on each other, stop criticising, stop finding fault.

You discover a fault you don't like in the person you wanted to marry. Don't you all have faults? Don't you all have weaknesses? Are not all of you failures? You condemn yourselves. I sympathise with weaknesses, but I have little sympathy for those who want sympathy for their weaknesses, but have no sympathy for the weaknesses of others. Love each other, people! Stop filling your mouths with sharp arrows and injuring each other. How can you love those in the world, if you cannot love each other?

Don't think of me as being harsh. I know my words are a bit tough, but if you need a surgeon, he is not going to bless you by patting you on the head. I am taking a knife to you, but I do it to heal you. My people are so contaminated by the world and it is time to wake up. My church is far from being the church I planned and it is time to wake up. It is time to put excuses away. It is time to look at yourself. It is time to look at my Holy Word and see how far you are from what it says. It is time to take seriously what I say in my Holy Word because, just as my Word can give life if you listen and act, so can the word of the world bring death if you listen and act. Most are listening and acting to the world and, my dear children, it is time that you stop!

Self-congratulations and the applause and approval of the crowd might make wrong feel right but it doesn't make it right. What I say is right is right, and what I say is wrong is wrong. It is high time that my children listen to their Father because these are dangerous times and you must listen to your Daddy. If I sound a little harsh, then you know it is seriously important and that I know what I am talking about.

On Authority

Authority is tough for you people to respect. This age is one where wives do not respect husbands, children do not respect their fathers and mothers, and there is little, if any, respect for teachers, political rulers, or police. The rules are up for grabs. You can consider them, debate them, and see if you like them first; then disobey them or try to change them. My rules are eternal. My Holy Word is in heaven and will be there eternally. Turn your back on it and pay the price; embrace it and receive its rewards. No man wrote it and no man is going to change it. Handle it with as much respect as you should have for me because my Holy Word and I are inseparable. The Word is Christ. Do not stumble over him. He loves you, has saved you, and wants to bring you home, if you will listen and permit him to work in his power in your heart.

A WORD TO THE CHURCHES

I hate the *corporate aspect* of the church—churches that boast of numbers, of fast growth, of wealth. Why? Who grants the increase if it is truly something spiritual and eternally beneficial? It is by the hard work of man that many churches grow today. Yet in the first century, it was good hearts being moved by the Holy Spirit via the preaching of my truth. What's changed? Well for a start, the truth is diluted and weakened.

Does a blunt sword of truth cut through to the heart as well as a sharp one? Does muddy and adulterated truth do the same job as my Holy Truth? If there is no difference, then why bother with the Scriptures at all? Oh no, that would be no good, would it? That would not be Christian. You would no longer be able to call yourselves a Christian church and that is important. Well, it's a pity that the Holy Word is not also important to you. How convenient that partial truth gives you whole Christianity. Why is the whole truth in the Scriptures if only part of the truth were needed? Surely I could have just put part of the truth in the Holy Word and you wouldn't have been any the wiser. How impudent that you choose parts—the bits you like—and leave the rest.

I have heard of churches that think it is okay to argue, to fight with their bothers, to despise them, to call them names, to talk behind their backs, to try to subtly malign them and undermine them—all in the name of Holy Truth. What a perverse group of people you are. You go to your seminaries and learn more Scripture to sprout, yet you neglect love for your brothers. It is no wonder you do not love your brothers—you don't love me—you don't love.

A WORD TO TEACHERS
AND LEADERS

Tuesday, February 19, 2013

I say to you now, think of something—anything that you will not give up, that you will not change—and I ask you why will you not give it up and why will you not change it? What hinders you? Is it the income from your church and the fear of, "What will I live on? How will I pay my mortgage and car loan? How will I pay my kids' school fees? How will I feed my children and my wife?"

Is it the embarrassment of what people will think if you lose your position, lose your church, lose your religion and all the friends and colleagues who look up to you and respect you—or that you may even lose your wife? Is it the thoughts of where do I go, what do I do, where do I worship? What group of Christians is out there doing it in a way that I, God, prescribed? Perhaps it is the thought of worshipping in a tiny group and beginning all over again, with no wages, and trying to create a church from scratch?

You are probably thinking, "This book is a load of rubbish. This is not God talking, but a man who hates comfortable churches and wants to unsettle what is still." Or you're thinking that the differences are tiny, miniscule—like playing politics, like leaving a little dot off an "i" or a cross off a "t"—pathetic little things that, if you have enough faith, God overlooks as not being as important as loving God and Christ. Well you are right there because nothing is as important as loving me and my Son, your Saviour; and this is exactly my point.

You love your churches, creeds, denominations, exclusivity,

inclusiveness, acceptance of everyone, the amount you give, your ministries and missionaries, your works of service, your qualifications, income, things, homes, cars, luxuries, education, beauty, bank balance, kids, wife, husband, parents, friends, families—more than me and my Son. You will not change anything for me and my Son. You will not change your heart and you will not let me get inside you to change your heart.

You have this huge clutter of stuff and you call it your beliefs, your religion. But it is false faith because it is faith that is not in me and in what I say, but rather in you and what you believe is okay. It is based on what your friends and those who agree with you think and on what those who you agree with think. It is a web of interconnected comfort that you are stuck to. It is inescapable. It has you trapped.

My truth sets you free; it doesn't trap you. My truth gives life by giving you myself, God. But your supposed truth keeps you from your God and your Christ. I know, you find this offensive and, because of your polluted hearts, you will dismiss this as coming from a deluded, lying crank—a mere man. Okay, go your way and think no more about it. You can be sure I will remind you of my words and your decision later.

For those who have ears—those whose hearts have not been made impenetrable by what you call truth, but which is not my truth—listen, for the days for listening are very short and very few. I have come into this world to separate friend from friend, to cut families apart, to drag one away from the other, so that I may have a few true hearts, faithful hearts—those who will listen to me.

Yes, I sympathise. Centuries of leaders teaching and preaching that "near enough is good enough", is sure to impact you. The standard setters have set no standard, for otherwise they would be measured and found wanting. Some will ask, but when did we preach "near enough is good enough"? No, you are right, but you taught it whenever you spoke your theology of compromise—expedient teachings that anyone with an honest searching heart could see the holes in—huge holes, big enough to drive trucks through and sail container ships through—more than big enough to make fools of yourselves and an even bigger fool of me.

Still I sympathise, for there was a strong temptation to comply, to do what every "good" and "faithful" Christian was doing, and just do it the same as they were. But, of course, it was still false, wasn't it? It was not based on faith in me, was it?

You are likely to be thinking, "but this cannot be God speaking, because this is critical of all the great reformers, the spiritual revolutionaries, who were listening to God, getting it right, teaching it, and living right." I have even more sympathy for those who are thinking this, because most reformers were moved by me and were doing their best, given the delusions, perversions, and adulterations to the truth that I was calling them to correct. But while some of the corrections made were from me, additions were also made that were new perversions; so it was a case of two steps forward and one step back. I can see with most variations and transformations, an overall progress back toward the truth taught by my Son and my apostles and my evangelists in the first century, but there is still much further to go.

To you, it does not appear much further to go but, trust me, you are deaf and blind to how far your truth is from my truth because your hearts are far from me. When you fall completely in love with me, you will hear how loudly I am crying out with the truth. You will see how clearly I am guiding you to a truth that is from, and has always been from, the throne of grace and only from the throne of grace. To say truth comes from a church is false. Truth only comes from me, God. Churches are simply the people who believe the truth as I taught it, and who live it because they love me.

Tell me the truth when you answer me: When I ask you, if a man was to say that you and your church are not keeping some aspect of truth, how would you take it? What would your reaction be? I'll answer for you so that your answer can be an honest and true one. You would consider him a troublemaker, a fault-finder, one who lacks loyalty, one who is divisive, and you would distance yourself from him. And so it has been for centuries whenever anyone has been prompted by my Holy Spirit to see and hear the truth and share it with others, including pastors, preachers, and others holding pastoral and shepherding positions.

Shepherds of what and for whom? I can best answer this one too. Shepherds of your own philosophies, for your own man-made churches, churches that hinder those who my Holy Spirit encourages to seek and search out places to be grown by faithful children of mine, children of the Most High God. Should I commend you? Would you like that? I would love to, for I love you all so dearly, but few of you know me.

Am I not sympathetic and do I not show it? For centuries I have found good hearts amongst Catholics and Protestants, and I have led them from where they were. These have loved me and followed me, and I have accepted their blindness, lack of knowledge, and their lack of the pursuit of my perfect truth because they loved me intensely. Their love was impressive and I love keeping company with people who hate their sins, who repent and weep over their sins, and who love me and find everything they have ever hoped for in me.

Some may accuse me of making it confusing—that by working in the lives of faulty people with faulty theologies, I was signalling that it was okay to get it wrong. All I can say is, how stiff-necked is a person, or churches filled with people, when they cannot read the truth and do it, when they cannot see how important obedience is? My Scriptures are there to show what pleases me and my Son, so that you may do what pleases me, be found in a close relationship with me, and be cleansed by the redeeming blood of my Son. Anyone who reads my Scriptures and cannot see my Scriptures as being important to me, is reading without comprehending. And if my Scriptures are important to me, surely they should be important to you, because they were written for you, not for me. I don't need Scripture. I am, in part, the Words that I say. But you need to know and obey Scripture so that you may be assured of eternal life.

My truth is important to me, and you getting it right is important to me, because my truth sets you free and gives you life. It is my truth, and your interest in it and transformation by it that goes a long way toward showing how much you love me, and how much you are changed by keeping company with me and my Holy Word.

Do you believe that my truth is the key to spiritual life? My Son told you that his words were life. The religious leaders of his day refused to listen and change, and they were judged for their hard hearts. My Son established his truth, his church, and no one drew high wages from it. None of my first century apostles or pastors saw it as a cushy career opportunity, but it is that for some today. Some pastors have set up churches that are sources of big earnings for themselves. Their money is their church. The Pharisees in Jesus day also carefully examined how they might change the way worship was practised with regard to giving and money, and they got rich. When Jesus came, his way was against their corruption. When it came to enticing the traitor, they used money. Those corrupted by money were corrupting others with money. Ministry is not about money. It is not about careers. It is not about qualifications or church-imposed or seminary-imposed rules and regulations. It is about people humbly approaching me, their God, walking and talking closely with God and Christ, and listening and doing as instruction comes from my throne of grace.

This is not about churches but about me, God—not about church power but about God power, my power—not about words and teachings of churches but about words and teachings of mine, of God. You have lost your way and your churches have become like deaf and blind guides to a deaf and blind god, like an idol made with human hands. Sad and ironic, but true. So it always is and so it always must be when even sincere people step away from me.

The ways of error are infinite, but the way of truth is but one, divinely one! Never think you have anything, unless what you have is me. Without me, without my Son, without my Holy Spirit, there is nothing worth having and nothing that will, in the end, leave you with anything.

The days are few, the path is being cleared. This is my broom that sweeps away the errors of churches, pastors, preachers, and priests so that my Son may approach and find good hearts, unhindered by man's error. Many think they know, but unless you see it written by me and I teach you its meaning, how do you know? Unless you hear from me, God, what do you have that is valuable for teaching the people? Or have you not read that my apostle Peter instructed that your words should be like the words of God. So do not teach anything that does not come from me.

If you are not hearing from me, do not teach. If you are not hearing from me, do not lead. If you are not hearing from me, you have not been called; for if I called you, you would know—you would have heard from me then and, at times, afterwards. My own Son did not speak on his own, but he spoke the words he heard from me. How much more do you think that applies to all of you? Or are you so deluded and puffed up that you are better than my Son, the Messiah? Humbly approach me, and if I have nothing to say to you, do not be offended. It is just that I have nothing for you to teach to others, Pray that I will place someone near to you, so that you may have someone to teach you—someone who is hearing from me.

Some are so arrogantly thinking that the first century letters and writings qualify you to teach, and that you do not need to hear from me. Allow me to become a little clearer, to help you, lest your belly take you to hell. Answer me this: Did my Son have any Scriptures? Obviously he did, yet the sharp sword of truth he wielded was guided by me and by my Holy Spirit. My Son was the Word incarnate; yet he was humbly guided past his physical lack, by me and the Holy Spirit, to make absolutely certain that every word he spoke was truth for you. How presumptuous of you to think that you are in a better position to teach than was my beautiful and radiant Son, the Holy Word in the form of a man. Take care, all those who aspire to teach and to lead, for if every word that you teach and every bit of leadership, direction and decision-making that you initiate does not first come from me, your Father, then it is from you and you are not authorised.

To those who have ears, eyes, and a heart for me, immediately disband your so-called churches. Meet for prayer together. Ask of me that I guide you into all truth. My Holy Spirit will be true to the Holy Word and will do that for you. Then, in plain view of everyone in your groups, open my Word on the floor, and open all your teachings on the floor beside my Holy Word. Leaving your church dogma, creeds, prayer books, rules and regulations, start fresh, with a new empty book, and begin writing down everything you see in my Holy Word that pertains to worship, to the churches, to moral living, to care for the poor and the lost, and keep writing until all my Holy Words are written down. Use these notes as a summary and as a map for your church to function and live by.

Do all these things in complete consultation with my Holy Spirit. Do not permit any error. If anything is unclear and my Holy Spirit does not declare it clearly, leave it, and proceed. If there is dispute over what the Holy Spirit is teaching, and it is clear that some people are saying what is clearly wrong, take no further word from those people. Choose the persons who will be given the responsibility of receiving the instructions from the Holy Word via prayer and the drawing of straws so that I, God, may be given the authority and position to make these choices, in order to avoid the snare of those who feel they are hearing from the Holy Spirit, but are not.

In this way, proceeding locally, no church shall be above another church, and churches shall function and be led by my Holy Spirit, with sensitivity to the local culture as to the manner and form of praise and worship of me, so that the hearts of my children are not hindered from drawing close to me when they come together.

To those who find fault with this servant, my scribe, know this: that those who found fault with the people chosen by me for a purpose have always done so according to the merit of their own failings; ask my Holy Spirit, who will give you full assurance. To those of you who, through familiarity with this servant, my scribe, despise him, know this of him: that you may not know him or accept him as a friend, but

I do. Your insults to him are your insults to me. Short of my Son, the Messiah, I do not choose the perfect, but the faulty, and I do not choose the whole, but the broken, for my glory shines bright though the vessel be ignoble. I am pleased to say that I know David, a man of gentle and lowly heart. When I change a man, he is changed. When I choose a man, he is chosen. When David asked me if I had a name that I wanted to name him, I told him, "Emmanuel."

He was shocked and thought he was deluded or being addressed by one who was blaspheming. I explained to him that the reason why he did not understand, was that his understanding was wrong, like that of so many today. Emmanuel should be the spiritual name of every believer in Jesus Christ because you are God to the people. You are people through whom God comes into the world— into the hearts and lives of the people. You should have the mind and the thoughts of Christ, and the words of Christ and the Holy Spirit on your lips. All saints are "Emmanuel", and if they cannot be called "Emmanuel", they are not in Christ.

Understand this: if you want to find faults in David, they are not hard to find. Heinous sins and crimes has he committed, but Jesus changes lives. Struggles, weaknesses and imperfections are present by the truck load in David; yet I love to be with him, for he knows and loves my heart, he knows and loves the heart of my Son, and he knows and loves the heart of my Holy Spirit. I love sharing with David. I adore his special heart. For those who want to accuse him and to despise him and to tear him down, know that his heart I encountered also in another David long ago, who also had faults, but who loved me with a rare and a special love. David loves me and I love him. Ask my Holy Spirit to confirm my meaning.

Do not allow personal offence to cause you to cling to your faults and not be released to grow and be blessed.

Most of you will use any excuse to avoid pulling down your high places. Your churches are your idols and will be to the end. Your love is for your churches. You will not give up your denominations, your names, your creeds and everything that distinguishes you and separates you from others. Do not take comfort in your interdenominational structures. A community of shared or exclusive error does not impress me. Pull it down. Disband and begin again. You cannot put a band-aid on a dying man and expect it to bring him back to life. Yes, my Son redeems; but he is not a supporter of error. Yes, I have patiently waited for further transformation, and a few of you are being moved by my Holy Spirit to do that, which is commendable. But do not think that it is a work for only a few. If you do not have a heart for transformation, stand aside and permit others to follow me. I will not deprive my little ones of my message and the blessings that go with it.

If leaders will not lead transformation, I will cause the least of my sons and daughters to rise up, to hear my voice, to answer my call, and return to the pure waters of the fountain that is the Holy Word of my teachings. I will bless those who listen to me and dispense to them my power, the power of revival. So many are calling out to me for revival, asking that I grant a new revival worldwide. This is a great petition but how do I encourage good hearts to come from a contaminated world into a contaminated church?

Many who read my words will discount them and consider themselves as unworthy of my blessings, growth, and revival. Yet they are in dead churches and wish and hope for something better from me, without lifting a finger themselves. A heart for me is a heart for change. What is not from me is in opposition to me and in opposition to you.

Some of you who hear these words of mine, will be in churches that believe they already have the truth—all the truth—and cannot change or transform to become anything better, but only worse. How deluded is a delusion that disqualifies from even an honest consideration of transformation and correction to lead back to the truth? If any church in so-called developed countries believes that it is the standard by which all other churches are measured, when did you ask me? When did you consult me? Humbly bring your teachings before me and I will show you your error and all that needs changing.

Do you think I do not know what truth is? Know this: that there is no man who brings to me a standard that impresses me. I have given you the standards, I have set them. No church in the developed world knows them or keeps them in whole. Everyone must change, get honest and sincere, and change for the love of me.

Others are drunk on the spirit, but are insensitive to my Holy Spirit and self-deluded. My Spirit is not one of confusion and disorder. I see people pushed to the ground by pastors who claim it is the Holy Spirit. Stop lying. I do not need your lies. It appals me when you tell me to heal on your command. I am not your God to be told what to do by you. Stop treating me like an idol, like a show ring master in a circus who is on your payroll to do your signs and wonders.

I heal those who I choose to heal for my glory, not for your glory. I heal and bless and impact the lives and the hearts of little lost lambs who need to know me as their Saviour, not you as their saviour. These are my children—not yours—redeemed and cleansed from their own sins, and destined for a home not made by your hands but by mine. Stop turning your supposed worship into sideshows. I am not your hired act. Stop trying to fill your churches with people who come to watch me perform and, when I don't do as I am told, you deceive the people with false miracles or with miracles that insult the intelligence of even your kids. It doesn't matter how you say it, how many times you say it, or how many of you say it—what is wrong is wrong—what is not from me is not from me.

The bigger the church, the longer the history, the greater the wealth, and all the harder it will be for you to give up all you have made and all you have placed your faith in from your own hands. If the pope stood up today and said he was transforming your Catholic churches and all would be made new in accordance with my words, you would kill him tomorrow. If leaders of the Church of England did likewise, you would run them out of town. I know the truth and I know how much of a burden you have placed on your own backs. I love you all, but do not expect me to bend my back and carry your burden that you have placed on your backs to bring you glory and greatness. Do you think that I will endorse and encourage you in your sin? I love you too much to do that.

Let's talk money. Why don't you trim your home church budget so that 90% of what my children give you goes into the kingdom to support evangelists in spreading my Word throughout the world and to relieve suffering throughout the world? Most church budgets greedily swallow up 80% of funds on ministers' payrolls and building expenses. It is a sick church that does that. It is not what the church did in the first century. Put my kingdom first and not your own. You know exactly what I mean. And if you are so far into denial, my Holy Spirit will guide you from your error and into holy budgets, if you will ask him and if you will do what he tells you.

LOVE THE SINNERS

Wednesday, February 20, 2013

I have seen churches that use fellowship and love like a weapon. If a person does not keep all the ways that please the group, they shun them. They don't tell them why they are giving them the "cold shoulder", as you commonly describe it. They make it clear that no longer will they receive a warm welcome with a smile, and no longer will they be received with an inclusive spirit but, instead, they are excluded from an inner circle of fellowship, a circle of fellowship that turns inwardly to favour the "good" and to exclude the "bad".

I extend fellowship to you. I never turn my back on you. Yet you do such things to your brothers and sisters. Don't you know that when you do that to your family members or your church members, you do that to me? You claim no creeds, but your churches are filled with creeds unwritten—evil creeds of hate and not fellowship. How can you, being evil, teach others to do good, when you practice evil and when you set examples that are evil? How can you ever bless and lift up those around you, and encourage higher and more worthy behaviour in your brothers and sisters, by having a low and worldly standard for your fellowship and love? Even the world sets examples of love that rise above that, with people who can love more than you can—even by their own power. How much more should you be loving, when it is by my power that you love? But you do not love because you do not know love. Yet I have loved you before you were born. Before I made the universe, I loved you. You are always loved by me. The very least you can do is love other evil and fallen people, as I love you.

I hear you use the teaching of my servant Paul, who commanded a sinning brother to be excluded from friendship and fellowship. When Paul took this action, he consulted me. It was my action. I took this action because immorality that is lifted up to be considered worthy, to be seen as good and right, is a perversion of the truth that will surely take people to hell, and I love too much to do that. I loved that misguided group of my children and I loved that misguided son of mine. I did it out of love. I did it by my power. Paul and the group prayed for that man to powerfully be brought to his senses and back into fellowship with me and with his spiritual siblings. But when you do it, it is done as an expression of your hate, unforgiveness, and wickedness. You sit there and pick on a sinner among you, who is often not as bad as you are. How can you do that, when you are loved by me and in fellowship with me? But this is key to your failure: you have a set of rules. You have a rule book. Yours is a club manual with members' rules. If members break the rules, they are out, or may as well be. You don't want them anymore. They don't measure up. You, as a group, reject them so they will wither on the vine. They will dry up and they will wander away from the flock because to be lost has more comfort and appeal than to be despised by a flock of hate-filled sheep.

What are you doing with my love and fellowship that I extend to you? Where are the leading sheep of the flock who encourage this? They are flock leaders who have no connection to the good shepherd, who do not value their good shepherd, who do not honour their good shepherd, who have learned nothing from their good shepherd who gives them everything and then deny other sheep. Know this: that my Son and I are not like you. Your sins cost us dearly. We know the price of cleansing you of your heinous sins. We are not petty or mean in generously giving forgiveness and love to our children, for we know the price, and the full price has been paid. Why do you meter out our love and forgiveness as if you paid for it, as if it cost you, as if it is running out and cannot be spared for the unworthy? Are you worthy? By your own actions you declare yourself worthy and others of your choosing, unworthy. Who made you God? When did you become perfect in conception and sinless from birth? There is no other God besides me and everyone who chooses to be me does not just make a bad god, but an evil and completely wicked god. Go away and learn for yourselves about love and fellowship and then extend it to your brothers and sisters generously. And stop using it as a weapon to force the members of your club to submit to your club rules.

You do this because you have no connection to the head, Christ. You are not in fellowship with me, the Father. If you were, you would walk and talk with me, you would ask me and, even if you neglected to ask me, I would tell you. I would tell you that you are wrong, that your behaviour is destructive, that you are destroying the blessing that my Son and I give to our children. We give them good things, while you take away the good things we give and, instead, give them your hate and coldness. No wonder some leave your churches and describe you as Bible-Nazis. Yours is a gospel of hate and your churches make welcome the nature of the devil, unleashing a spirit of hate, and locking up and keeping from my children my Spirit of loving forgiveness. I speak to you and I correct you from doing this. But you have decided, in all your great wisdom, that God doesn't do that anymore—that I do not speak—that I am no longer in fellowship personally amongst my children.

How can I, a loving Father, not be found amongst my children? How can you, who call yourselves children of mine, who say you run the true and correct churches, the best churches, the superior churches, look down your noses despising others, while you meter out your doctrines of hate and condemnation? There is not a word that is serious enough to use to express how vile this is or how angry and frustrated I feel when I look at your behaviour. I attend to the healing of all those you have cut down and maimed and injured by your theology that you have intellectualised and formularised. To you, I no longer exist and am no longer central and honoured. But you yourselves are central. You must be obeyed or else—while my teachings about my Holy Spirit, about my power, and about my love and forgiveness are ignored.

You despise me when you act like this—when you set up your churches according to the spirit of man and not according to my Holy Spirit. Choose now whom you will worship: me or yourself? I have removed your lampstands. Your churches are shrinking and failing. You despise my power, so I have removed my power from your churches. You have despised my love and lifted up your rules, so your churches are impoverished of my nurture and healing. I will humble you and bring you to your knees to make you cry out to me for answers that you do not have, to cry out for love and fellowship that you do not have. Come before me humbly and ask of me, listen to me, know my voice, and do what I tell you so that you may be blessed, for you are arrogant and pitiful.

Oh, how I love you. Oh, how much I long for the day when you will love the Lord your God with all your heart, soul, mind, and strength, and your neighbour as yourself. Oh, how I long for you to write my words on your hearts and not just on your lips. Know me, taste me, break apart your clubs and enter into the feast of fellowship with me, your Father God. Repent and present yourselves for forgiveness and cleansing so that I might fill you with every spiritual blessing, so that pure water may flow from my throne of grace, through you, and out to all the people. I love you. Go in my power and my strength as you change, and love one another as I love you.

PEACE, LOVE AND HOPE

Wednesday, February 27, 2013

Faith hijacked—hijacked faith! Why are all extremists violent and hateful? Why are all extremists not seen as extremely loving, kind, and compassionate? Where have peace, love, and hope gone? Why have many churches lost these qualities or why are they seen by so many to have no qualities or answers when it comes to these questions? Almost every sane person on the planet wants peace, love, and hope, regardless of whether they believe in God or not. But most people no longer see Christian churches, Jewish temples, or Islamic mosques as being the place to go to find them, to learn about them, or to find people living as examples of peace, love, and hope that others can learn from. Religion has lost its key appeal, its key point, its key difference and uniqueness because it has lost the "love your neighbour as yourself and do to others as you would like done to you" Attitude. Of course, we see in the Jewish Torah, the Christian Old Testament and the New Testament, the teaching: "Love the Lord your God with all your heart, mind, soul, and strength, and love your neighbour as yourself." Jesus said to the Pharisees and the crowds that this was the summation of all the Mosaic Law and the writings of the prophets.

So it is that, in losing this, you have lost loving God, your neighbour, and yourself as being the heart of your beliefs, and have replaced it with your churches, your creeds, your interpretations, your sectarianisms, your hatred and despising of others, and your acceptance of others based upon whether they completely agree with you or whether they do not agree with you. You have thrown out what is at the heart of the matter: love for me—your God, for others, and for yourself. You have set up your separate theologies as gods that divide and despise. Your churches effectively spit in the eye of your God and of others and, just as effectively, you spit in your own face.

Where is Christ? Where is my love for you, my children? My redeemed ones, those I love, my children, have pushed others away with their rejection and hate. I love you and I called you to me, overlooking your shame and the stench of your filth, and I told you to do the same for others. But instead you have hated and rejected. I taught you love and peace but you have perverted my words into practises that excuse violence. You have found ways to excuse your hatred using my words. You twist my teaching to support your evil ways and horrible treatment of others. I condemn you for this.

But hear this, my children: Because I am not like you, I love you and I save you. In my compassion, I save you. I overlook your blackest sin. And now I tell you to overlook the sin you find in others. But do not overlook the sin of your yoke and the weight of your load that you have placed on them. They have not sinned by disobeying your introduced theology of pride and lording it over others. Repent, I implore you.

My return is so soon. How old are you? How much older will you get before I return for you? Are you ready? No, I say you are not ready. Lay aside all that hinders, cast aside your interpretations that trample my so-called "golden rule", for you have made it far from golden; you have made it so it cannot be recognised.

Who are you following? Who has bewitched you? I know that centuries of creeds have dulled my message of love. I understand that this has made you drunk in your confusion. If you love me, you will keep my commandments. And my commandment is this: that you love one another. Greater love has no man than he who lays down his life for another and someone may dare to love with such a love. I ask you, would you lay down your life for an enemy because of your love? Yet, you have made enemies of your brothers. Will you love your brothers, who are now your enemies, with a love that makes you want to lay down your life for them? My little children, whom I died to save, love your brothers, love your enemies, and remove your evil creeds that have made enemies of your brothers. Remove your names that separate. Remove your traditions and customs that separate.

FOLLOW ME AND LOVE OTHERS

I weary of your hindrances. I did not place these burdens on your backs. I did not make your yokes harsh and cruel, children. When I said, "Follow me," I did not mean follow a bit of me and lots of you. I meant, "Follow me." What sort of disciple are you? My disciples follow me. When you do not follow me, you are not my disciple. Am I not your Rabbi? Am I not your super-Rabbi—your Rabbi with authority, who bought you as my disciple with my blood and saved you so you can thrive in the blessings and richness of my words of life now and, in the near future, reside with me forever? Are you ready to go? Is your work finished?

Have you ensured that everyone knows I love them, and I saved them, and I want them in heaven with me forever; and that all they have to do is seek my heart, fall in love with me and with my Father? No, you have thrown books at them, not lavished them with my patience and love, as I do you. You convert them to a church, to a faith, to a religion. You do not introduce them to me or to my Father. You give them rules. You make sure that they are not divorced, or homosexual, or a thief, or a smoker, or a drinker, or a gambler, or a dancer. You introduce them to a set of rules. You have introduced them to a Pharisee, not to me. You have introduced them to someone who is itching to find some reason to reject them, with something to teach them, with something to correct them. Worst of all, you called your abomination of faith godly! How dare you? Repent now. Fall at my feet and weep in deep sorrow for breaking my heart. I am not the one you have taught others about. I am filled with love.

I am the one criticised and despised for essentially teaching that my love is enough. My words have life, not yours. Your words kill. Stop your teaching and learn more correctly my words of love. Yes, there is correction. Yes, there is morality. Yes, there are standards. What do you first teach your own babies, your own little ones? You teach them that they are loved. You expect nothing of them until they know how much they are loved by their daddies and their mummies. You have not done that for my little ones. Do you know how much I love you? Let me remind you here and now that, no matter how much you have sinned against me—no matter how much you have perverted my teachings and have not lived them as I instructed you—I still love you, I still save you. Do you know how much I forgive you? Before you speak again to another living soul, go to a quiet place and contemplate your huge and horrendous sins, then come back to me with a sorrow-filled and contrite heart, full of desire to change who you are. Come home to my arms for you are the prodigal. Simple, humble, heartfelt repentance is all I ask—a natural response to how much you are loved by me.

I am empty of your love. You have set up your church against me, your teachings against me. You have unwittingly made your theologies more a friend to Satan's work than to mine. How tragic, how pathetic, how fallen you are. Yet I cannot help but adore you. I cannot stop cherishing you. I cannot fail to love you for I am love and, when I love you, I am simply being me. Go away and learn this. My disciples learn to love as I love. They learn to be God in bodily form, as I was. They learn to be Emmanuel, as I am. Do you want to be my disciple? Love one another as I have loved you. Stop hindering my kingdom and tarnishing my unblemished name with your manifold reasons found to defame and despise others.

Show me your change of heart. Show me your repentance. Here is a name for you: Christchurch! Show me your oneness in your name. Show me your fellowship with all who seek to gather to worship and adore me, with all who come for my balm of Gilead, for all who assemble to praise and worship with you. Do not ask them what they believe, or what church they are from, or where they attended in the past, for the past is gone and all things are made new. This is a new beginning. A new star rises in the sky—a clear and bright star. Look up, not at each other.

Break down your structures and your systems of management. Throw them away for they have harmed much. Choose new leaders—spiritual men of God—whom the Holy Spirit appoints. Seek the Holy Spirit's counsel, let him choose, let him decide. Use straws or any methods that give God the privacy to act decisively. Allow your God to rule. Place me back on the throne over my church. Give back what is mine. Give back what you stole from me. She is my bride and I am the only one who died to redeem her. Look to the letters for advice on your structures and, where nothing is stated, you are free to choose, based upon prayer and the guidance of men who are in conversation with the Holy Spirit. Any man who does not know what I mean need not be placed in a position of trust in the kingdom, until he does. If a man wants wisdom, knowledge and understanding, ask me.

The Lord Jesus Christ says: I am taking back my church and the leadership of my children whom I love, for I am the Way. It is my words that give life; it is my blood that saves. No longer shall there be arguments about the day of worship. Worship is the first day of the week. No longer shall you debate and pervert baptism. Baptism is by full emersion and is the commencement of your rebirth in God, your God-in-the-flesh life. Any thoughts about baptism are simply knowing what to do and doing it. No longer will you sprinkle babies or adults, and no longer will you put baptism off for days or decades. About praise, whether it is with musical accompaniment or as a capella, if it is coming from a heart filled with love for me and is done to worship me, it is acceptable. David's praise with musical instruments and choirs was and is accepted by me.

Remember my death, burial, and resurrection every time you meet. Holy water, the sign of the cross, prayer books, various chanting, confession to and forgiveness of sins by priests must stop. Through my apostles, I gave to my children a simple way to worship, filled with freedom and liberty, but you have distracted them with all your traditions that are not my traditions.

Nevertheless, leaders must teach the truth in love, with full patience and compassion; do not force. Ask the Holy Spirit for ways to remove the old man-made traditions and to only have the teachings from me. You are to remove all man's traditions from your main assemblies so that my teaching is above and over all. If there are any who cannot leave behind all the old man-made traditions, the leaders should meet with them separately and away from main meetings. The Holy Spirit should be petitioned, with loving and patient prayers, so that all my children willingly adopt and embrace my teachings fully, without taking from or adding to them.

If you love me, you will do as instructed. Love one another. Part of love is submission to my commandments. The church leaders, appointed by me, will teach the truth in love. So it is that you will not force anyone to do anything that they cannot agree to or do not understand. Instead, you will love them and pray for them, and petition for knowledge to be revealed to them from the Holy Spirit. And until that day comes, you will extend to them my patient love and my fellowship, and tenderly nurture their faith, and you will trust me to teach and to lead my little ones to knowledge.

David, let me speak to you for a moment. "Yes, Lord," I said. Do you recall when the rich young ruler asked me what he had to do to be perfect? "Yes, Lord". What did I tell him? "You told him that, if he wanted to be perfect, he should sell all he had, give it to the poor, and follow you." That's right, David. Did he? "No, Lord, he didn't." What was he really saying? "You invited him to be one of your disciples and he was saying, 'No.'"

David, his decision was obvious because he walked away. Today, many are in churches worshipping me every Sunday. They have not walked away but they are not my disciples because their hearts have never come near to me. In their hearts, they are not my disciples. Their bodies may indicate that they are, but they are not. My disciples are my disciples in the body and from the heart. It is too easy for people to call themselves Christians and to attend church every week. They think they have done all to get to heaven, but the doorway to heaven is through my heart, David.

Disciples are first and foremost disciples because they love and adore me. They want to know everything I think, and say, and do, so that they can be just like me—just like the one they love. Being Christian is not ticking a box, it is falling in love. Yes, I understand there is a process to falling in love. It takes certain knowledge. It takes spending time together. But chatting together and chilling out together is not really why a couple falls in love with each other. It is rather that, during the chatting and chilling out together, they click—they enjoy being together—and this enjoyment grows and grows until they don't ever want to be apart.

This is what Christianity is to me, David. A Christian is someone who cannot bear to be apart from me. And I can guarantee that they will never be apart from me in this life, or the next, eternally. I am serious about love, David. I am serious about the people I fall in love with and the people who fall in love with me. I reject no one who loves me. Everything that matters in this life brings you closer to me. The church matters, Scripture matters, teaching and learning and preaching matter, fellowship matters, Christian friendship matters—when they bring you closer to me. So it is that, if you are being taught by those who are not close to me, or if your church is led by men who are not close to me, or if your closest friends are not close to me, don't be so close to them. Everything that is close to you and everyone who is close to you needs to be close to me, so you are surrounded by every encouragement to approach the throne of grace with confidence. Be close to me, my Father, and the Holy Spirit.

Know who your Rabbi is; be around people who know who their Rabbi is. When you rise in the morning, when you eat, when you walk or work, do all things with your Rabbi. Be constantly in fellowship and harmony with your Rabbi. Always be asking me questions, always be discussing Scripture with me, always be asking for a second opinion on your thinking and attitudes so that you know, in every little area, what pleases me. In this way, you will become like me, and that is what a disciple is: he is like me. Any version or teaching about Christianity that is not personal and about a walking and talking relationship with me, and the Father, and the Holy Spirit, is false and not of God. If you do not know God personally and you are calling yourself a Christian, you do not know anything.

Now, I am not discounting that it can take months and years to walk and talk with me, just as it takes months and years to truly know any human friend. But an interest from the heart drives you forward—it makes you an explorer and one who wants to know everything about the one you are falling in love with. Your life is never the same when you are in love—madly in love—with someone. It is distracting and hard to get the one you love out of your head. So it is with Christianity. If theology or memorisations of Scripture were all it was about, the academics would find a perfect life an easy thing to attain. If being philosophical brought closeness to God, all those who fancy themselves as philosophers would be very holy. If it were about doing all the stuff right, perfectionists and the disciplined would be advantaged. If it were about getting the songs right, then the musically-gifted would be advantaged. Instead, it is the lovers who are advantaged—particularly those who are empty, hurting, hungry and thirsty to be loved. It is the humble, who consider themselves to be nothing, and nobody, and undeserving who will be surprised and delighted to be welcomed into friendship with me.

Those who think they have a lot and are able to make themselves happy are hard to impress and hard to please. Wealth and privilege disadvantage because they can give you the attitude of deserving it—deserving my love—and even deserving more. In that case, I am not enough and neither is my love. It is as if I didn't know how to please and as if I were not good enough. Like the rich young man who approached me. He loved his money. Money can do that. Instead, it was the poor and the disregarded in my society who embraced me.

The rich and the poor were eagerly awaiting my arrival. But the rich expected me to embrace them—I had to measure up to them—I had to follow them and make them my rabbi. Whereas the poor and disregarded did not expect to be received, and my love and my grace delighted them, and they came into fellowship with eager hearts. Sure, they had lots of growing and changing to do, and I challenged everyone who would listen and act on my words. But after I rose and it was clear that the Messiah had come, they followed me, regardless of the religious establishment hating, despising, and rejecting me.

WORSHIP THE ONE TRUE GOD

David, for thousands of years, I have contended with societies that have raised up their own imagined gods. They introduced fear, suffering and cruelty, they carved and made their gods with their own hands, deified them with their own imaginations. Demons seized the opportunity in some cases, encouraging incantations and evil meditations to bring supernatural power into some pagan worship. Man loves creating god, but because it is impossible to create God, man is left with the reality of having created nothing. At best, a union with demons was made, but nothing that is a blessing of love, peace, and kindness now, nor for life eternal. The eternal God is the only one who can offer eternal life, for he is the only one who has eternal life to offer. Nevertheless, man prefers the creation of imagined gods, rather than to worship the one and only true God and Creator of all life and the whole universe.

Today, those who know nothing, speak confidently about all religions being equal. This is false. They speak of all gods being equal. This is false. They speak of deity, by any name, as being equal to the one true God. We are not comparing different cars or different houses here. You can see what you are talking about and you can talk about something that is man-made, but how can you talk about the one true God who is without beginning or end—the Maker that human eyes cannot see? I reveal myself through my Word and man says, "I don't believe you; your teaching is as good as the teaching of a god born of man's imagination." What am I to do to cause man to believe in me? Is creation not enough evidence that the one great God created?

They see similarities in the worship of my sons, Abraham, Isaac, and Jacob, to the worship of the pagans around them, and they say, "See, it is similar because they are imitating pagan religions." They conveniently disregard the reality that it is as it is written because I taught humans how to worship and how to please me after they sinned and were driven from the garden. This information was passed down from generation to generation, with perversions added. And so it is that similarities exist for good reason, for each of their forefathers were taught by me to worship me. It is always the same, David. I create worship but man cannot leave it alone. They have to add to it, they have to take from it, they have to destroy it. They know better than me. So it is, even with my bride, my church—they tamper, change, adjust, modify, leave out, add, call one thing important and another unimportant and unworthy to be mentioned or practiced as it is written.

Where is my pure bride today? What have they done to her? They have dressed her in clothes I do not recognise. They have given her names I do not recognise. They have milked her for their own wealth, for their own pleasure, for their own popularity, fame, and position. She is humbled, confused, disgraced, mocked, and ridiculed. She is fought over by leaders who want high positions for their glory. She is fought over by women and homosexuals who want to seize her and make her bow to their petty concerns. Where is there a man who will stand up for my concerns? David, my church is a mess and I cannot recognise it. They don't recognise right from wrong and, when they argue their issues, I am not uppermost in their minds, but their traditions and reputations are.

This is why I write now. This is why I warn now. Does anyone have eyes to see and ears to hear? Does anyone know what truth is? Will anyone hear my voice, turn from their ways, repent and worship me as it is written? I am coming soon. Why be found ashamed? Why be surprised that I am not pleased? Listen now to what I have to say, and please me now, so that I may come and find my radiant church that I can recognise, know, and love. Repent, change, transform. You know you are in the last days.

So many of you are proudly speaking about having the Holy Spirit and many talk about speaking in tongues. Where is the benefit? Where is the truth? Is anyone listening? Is anyone asking? I would rather you spoke in your own tongue and worshipped and practiced in spirit and in truth, than speak in tongues. My sons and daughters have work to do—simple, basic, and practical work—to get back to what I taught. Do everything in love, patience, and in prayer.

JESUS, FRIEND OF SINNERS

Friday, March 1, 2013

My churches today are like the Pharisees when I came. You have made it hard and complicated, or you have made it easy with no rules for your friends. Either way, it is about your friends and you are either in or out of friendship with each other. The Pharisees built for themselves a church of power—their power; the power to decide who was in and who was out, the power to make the rules, the power to change the rules, the power to say everyone else's rules are wrong, the power to declare one person saved and another damned, and the power to declare whose groups of churches are saved or damned. How dare you? What do you know? Are you God? Yes, you think you are God. You are acting like God, but you are very horrible gods—gods without hearts or souls or mercy—gods without kindness. Do you think you are imitating me? Do you think you impress me? Do you think closeness with me is to come with pompous claims and deluded arguments to support your error? Repent, I say, and humble yourself and listen to me.

Who was I when I came? How was I when I came? I came as a friend, but not to all. I gladly accepted and came alongside the confused, the sad, and the fallen. The stench of their sin was all over me but it was the perfume of my righteousness that was all I could smell. Because of the company I kept, they called me a sinner, a friend of Satan, no friend of God. The company I kept was so often the very people that the church leaders of my day rejected outright. Those church leaders had no idea who they were rejecting. They did not know them, they did not know their hearts, they did not love them, and they would not call them friend. But I was prepared to not only keep company with them and teach them, but to become their friend. A friend is what the lost need.

You grade someone's beliefs according to your own beliefs, according to your own standards, but deep inside you, I know that my Holy Spirit rejects and troubles your heart for this. Your churches have become little better than clubs with club rule books. If you cannot agree on the rules, you are out of the club. How many souls have you damned to hell that I have transformed for heaven? Change and change quickly, so that I may come as a friend and not as an enemy. How can you act like me when you do not know me? Do you call me friend? What is a friend? I do not know you as a friend, but I want to and I died to. You are saved, and I have come to be a friend, but you and I are not friends yet. Friends spend time together and get to know each other. Friendship is real. Friends are real. All I am to you is a book of rules—no friend there. Friends, please understand that the Word, my Word, is a guide, a light, to lead you to close communion with me. If you follow it, you will not refuse me your friendship, your fellowship.

BE ONE AS WE ARE ONE

I was Rabbi to my disciples on earth. I left, telling them to wait for my Holy Spirit. My Holy Spirit came and mentored, guided, and counselled my disciples and all who have come since into friendship with me. If you have my Holy Spirit, you have both me and the Father. You have it all, you have us all. You are the ones holding back. You get my words and turn it into your book, a book without power. If I am your Rabbi, be my friend. Do everything with me. Be like me. Do everything like me. Spend your days and your nights beside me. Be my friend. You have set up your churches with different names, with different creeds, with different rules—club rules—to show who is a club member and who is not. How can all of you be following the same Rabbi when you all believe something different—when you all separate to go to "your" different church on a Sunday? Where do I go? What have you done? What have you done to the church of your Rabbi?

Your churches are an offence to me. The spirit that lurks within your churches opposes me. You say, "But we are not like that anymore." Yes, I realise I sent my servant, Billy Graham, to you and, in many practical ways, he set up for you an inter-denominational union. It was a step—a good step. Is it unity? No. Are you unified? No. Is there a worldwide group of followers who only call themselves Christians? No. Individually, you call yourself a Christian but collectively you are Baptist, or Catholic, or Anglican, or Pentecostal, or Methodist, or Presbyterian. Am I divided? No. Do you resemble the unity found in God when you cling to separate thinking? Why do you grasp to find something special in churches, something special in a name, something you feel is better in practise? Am I not enough? Do you come to worship me or do you come to worship your separate and unique practises? Where am I in your special practises? Do you do them for me? No. It is for you that you do them, not for me. You make yourself feel more comfortable. It is the way you like it. You like YOUR Christianity.

Throw off the burden of your differences that divide. Be one as I am one. My disciples had one Rabbi and I am he. Today you think you know, but you do not. You are deluded amid your differences. When I said to those I chose, "Follow me!"—some did and some didn't. It was my choice to ask, and it was their choice to follow or not to follow. Are you following me? No. Am I being harsh? Yes. I am being harsh because so many of you are so sincere, so genuine, and so conscientious in your confusion. You have been raised in a church culture where it is okay to pick and choose. You can change your Rabbi's skin colour and make him handsome to look at. You can make him cool and acceptable. You can change the way he thinks, give him new tastes, interests, likes, and dislikes. And most of all, you can make him like you and your church as the best of all. I am not your Rabbi who will change into one who lets you take over—who lets you teach him or correct him—a Rabbi who follows you after you set him straight. Can't you see what you have done? Can't you see what you are doing? You have made yourself the rabbi; you are god.

Now can you see why I must be harsh with you, why I must shock you, slap you with my words, shake you up and insult your confident smugness? Your confidence is not in me, but in yourself. Your confidence is not in the cross, but in your churches and their different teachings and creeds—you have chosen to follow one of them and declare that your saviour. I come as your faithful friend, your humble Saviour, to plead with you to see the error of your ways—the error of every Christian's ways—and to change you. Come to me. Come close.

Slow your life down. Turn your TVs off. Turn your music off. Make still your surroundings. Give to me one or two quiet hours of your day. During that time with me, please be my guest and chat, tell me all about what you want, and like, and what troubles you. But also ask me what I want, and like, and what troubles me, and what I have to say to you. Ask me what you should be reading, viewing, and listening to, so that you may be enriched and nourished spiritually. Remember, I am the Way, so I know the way. I am your mentor and guide. Do not be confused by books written by men. Ask me what to read. As you read Scripture, be humble and ask me to tell you and to show you what it means. As you read books, or listen to or watch sermons, ask me if the writer or preacher is correct and if it is for you.

You are my children but each of you have strayed and gone your own way. All of you have built your faith on yourself and your churches and not on me alone. If this were not true, I would not tell you. The Jews were often warned for decades, and sometimes for centuries, before correction came, and that showed our loving and kind patience. In the case of Christians, my Son, my Holy Spirit and I have demonstrated our loving and kind patience for nearly 2,000 years. But if we do not call you to repentance—if we do not correct—then we do not love, and to not love is impossible for us. Ask me, ask the Father, ask the Holy Spirit if these things are not true and you will know; we will confirm it true.

The truth is that time is short. I am appearing to senior Jews and Islamists but their people are not listening or responding. They think it cannot be me, it cannot be coming from the Christ, and it cannot be true. Nevertheless, it is true. I am calling to you Christians through a nobody, a nothing, a no one. But you have someone to ask, someone to confirm it. You have me and I will confirm my words and correction because I love you. Whether you believe, repent, and change now or later, that is up to you. My warning is clear. The days are short. You have been warned to be ready for my coming. You have the prophets who have told you of signs and these signs are now. The challenge goes out to you from me. Will you choose to not make waves, to not risk a falling out with your friends, to not upset your church leaders, or will you choose me and choose to follow me?

When I came to earth, many who followed me, who listened to me, were those who were already rejected and despised by the teachers and preachers of the day. Those who the religious people of my day rejected, I accepted. Those who the Pharisees would never have as a friend, I did. That cost me. The Pharisees used my friends as one of their reasons for rejecting me as their God. Through a nobody, a nothing, a no one, but a friend of mine—one who is despised and rejected by men, but a friend of mine—a man who has rejected the teachings of men but has accepted mine—through this man, I call you now. Will you listen to my call? Will you listen to my words?

BE MY FRIEND

The choice is yours to make. The decision is yours to make. If you call yourself a friend of mine, please do not make such a decision alone; ask me, ask my Holy Spirit, ask Father God. You do not know, but we do. Therefore, for any man or woman who does not hear my voice, does not know my voice, or is not in continuous communion with me, and the Holy Spirit, and Father God, this is your first task: walk and talk with me. Make me your closest friend. Let me be your Rabbi. Follow me. I will show you the way and I will guide you into all truth. I offer to you my heart of friendship. A heart filled with the most thrilling of friendships, both for now and eternity. I am the gentlest, kindest, sweetest, most tender and understanding friend, and I am filled with the greatest love and compassion for you. This is personal. I love you. I want you to enter into the deepest and most meaningful friendship there is. Without you in my heart, without you in my arms, I am not complete. Without you in heaven, heaven is not complete.

The time is short; there is much to change. Please come and let me shape you and change you. My Father kneads and shapes the clay of your heart, so that you may be the pot that can be used for his thrilling purposes for your life in my kingdom. There is a powerful enemy. The war is won, but battles blaze on. I want you shaped by me, not by the devil. Please recognise that you have stains in your thinking. They mar the clay of your heart and your life. They impede your usefulness to the conquest of the kingdom. Please hand over your life and your heart to me. Please do not fear me. I only want the best and I only have the best for you.

When was the last time someone truly sat down to study my Word, only my Word? When was the last time someone sat down to remove all the preconceptions that come to mind—all the excuses—all the reasons why it doesn't matter anymore? Be the first; but you cannot do it alone. You can only get it right with me. I am not telling you to use truth as a weapon of division. If you follow me, you will know forgiveness—you will know my heart and you will know peace, love, kindness, patience, and not taking offence. My truth unites. My truth unifies. My truth is a united front of love against the united front of hate, which lies in front of my victory and glory. Please be part of this.

Friends fight alongside each other, not against each other. When David stepped out to face Goliath, no mighty man of Israel—no strong and trained man of war—stepped out. All the army of Israel could have stepped out together but no one wanted to step out alone. That was their problem. They felt alone. That was David's strength. He did not step out alone. He knew that I would not let a young, believing heart stand without his best friend. The quiet months and years that David spent in the hills, tending his father's sheep, served him well. He became friends with me. I grew his faith. He encountered things with me that were too big for him to overcome alone. He knew that he was not alone because of the way he was able to protect his father's sheep from bears and lions. He knew he was not alone because he knew he was only a small, young man, not a mighty man.

Ironically, Israel's trained mighty men were not able to be used in my service on the day I had arranged to be Goliath's last day because all they could see was Goliath and they could not see me as their closest friend and mightiest of all defenders. Instead, I chose a young man who knew that he was weak but who also knew that I am invincible. One weak man, trusting in my close friendship and infinite power, and Goliath didn't stand a chance. Have you noticed what else happened that day? That day was the beginning of warriors. Mighty men of legend were made that day. Men were inspired. They saw what David did and they knew it was God; they knew it was me. I inspired many men that day to become heroes for my Israel. When men so dearly and truly want to believe in something more than themselves, and want to see me work my power, they don't just want to believe, but they want to be a close friend too, and see my power working to bring about my will.

Today I call out, through my words written in this book, to all good hearts across this globe. It does not matter to me what the colour of your skin is, nor whether you are very young or very old, whether you are male or female, whether you are trained for ministry or unschooled, whether you are wealthy or poor, whether you are healthy or poor of health, whether you are a prisoner or ex-prisoner, whether you are married or single, whether you struggle with weaknesses or are a sinner. My call is to you today. Draw near to me in quiet hours. Consult with me. Come into best friendship with me. If you cannot hear me, ask me for spiritual sensitivity so that you will receive into your mind, my thoughts. Learn of me. Learn my truth. Meditate on my Word. Read my Scriptures. Let me help you to understand how simple my gospel is.

Yes, there is sin. I died because of sin. Of course I hate sin. Sin is a killer, a destroyer, something of Satan. But you have my truth to teach you what I hate and to show you what I love. You have my power to enable you to overcome your weaknesses. You have my love that gives you strength. Anything that flows from Scripture and that does not cause behaviour that you saw in my life while I was on earth, is flawed. There is one truth. There are many ways to emphasise one truth over another. This brings a distortion, resulting in thinking and practises that are not truth. I am the God of order and balance. The truth that I will guide you to never disagrees with what is written, and will have the balance that only comes from me—a balance filled with mercy and grace, compassion and kindness. How can a word come from me that tosses my little ones away as if they were garbage? That is no truth of mine. The price I paid—the pure life I laid down—was for you and for your filthy sin. All of you sin. What you call righteousness is filth. You do not know what righteousness is. You do not know how filthy your sins and failings are in my sight.

As I choose to not rub your noses in your filth, do not rub the noses of those around you in their filth. I alone am righteous. Approach others in both truth and love. Teach and uphold the truth, in season and out of season, but love everyone as I have loved you. My truth, without love, is not my truth. I know your sin. I died for it. I know who you are. I know all your temptations, all your evil imaginations, all your pompous thoughts, your greed, your lack of faith, and all your lack of righteousness. And yet, I adore you and I love you. I cannot get enough time with you to satisfy my desire for you.

From morning when you rise until evening when you close your eyes to sleep, I am near— waiting for your mind to notice a single little thought of me, hoping to distract you to notice me, to think of me, have a thought of love for me, to stop and want to spend a moment with me. I spend my day always ready to stop—to drop everything— to spend time with you. I get off on you. You are my precious little child. I loved you before the universe was formed. I waited and waited to meet you, to see you. I long for closer and closer friendship with you—for more and more time with you—one-on-one—just you and me—best friends—like lovers—hearts that beat as one.

BE MY LOVER

I cleanse you, purify you. I see you sin. I watch the disgusting things you do. I hear the sick things you say. I know the horrible things you think. But I love and cherish you. I adore you and I cannot get enough of you. Slowly I see change, very slowly.

Now, the time is very short. Change must come quicker. To come close to me now is to be prepared to come close to me when you see me in the clouds of heaven. My heart melts for you. I have a bad case of love sickness for you. I long for you to have a heart that melts for me. I long for the day that you share a bad case of love sickness for me, and that you become as madly and passionately in love with me as I am with you, longing to spend eternity in my arms with me.

You were made for love. You were made for my love. You were made for heaven. You were made to be a child of God's family in heaven. Nowhere else will you be happy. Nowhere else will you belong or feel at home, than in your Father's house. I treasure every tiny moment that you allow me to spend with you and I wait impatiently for heaven—for my Father's call—when it will be time to return to gather the children and bring them home. Oh, how much I am eagerly waiting to see your face as you see mine, in my glory, and to share all I have with you, to take you to my Father. There is no word to say how you and I will feel then. Don't let Satan, don't let man, don't let theology, and don't let churches take that away from you.

CALL TO A LOVE REVOLUTION

I call into your heart right now. I am calling into your heart with these words of mine. I challenge you with these words: "Lead my revolution; where you stand in your strength, I will be with you." The hearts to whom this is given to hear have heard and, even now, are rising up. This is the revolution of all revolutions; this is the revival of all revivals. The hour is coming and has come. The completion of all is so close. I am so excited that my heart bubbles with joy. Rise up. Lead. Follow me. Rise up in the strength you have. Walk in close friendship with your Rabbi. Be at peace with me, be one with me, trust me, learn from me, have faith in me, receive my strength and power from me, and walk in my will.

As I have called you, call out to those around you. Gather them together in your home. Open my Word and learn from me. Learn from no one else—learn from me. Follow no one else—follow me. I am with you. I am for you. I am nearer than your nearest friend. I am closer than your closest friend. I love you more than any of your friends. Humble yourself before my Holy Spirit and seek his counsel. Listen for his thoughts as he steers you to truth. Take confidence, take heart. I steer you along a straight course. With all that man has added and thrown out of my Word, he has not set a straight course for you. Where man has failed, where even sincere men have failed, I never fail. Take heart; step forward with me. Inspire others as you are inspired by me.

A dark cloud has hovered over the churches for too long. Now the clouds will be forcefully removed. The Son shall shine and nothing shall hinder him from shining brightly into all the world. The shadows of the last 2,000 years will soon pass and the light will shine into the darkest areas of my kingdom.

To all those called by me to devote your life to my service far from your homeland, I know your sincerity and your sacrifices for my name. Your days of labour are soon to end. Take care what you teach. Re-examine my words. Take care what you call yourself and how you practise. I know you love me. Talk to me about these things. Rise up in truth and love where you are. Together, let's have the truth in love—and only my truth in love—taught and practised in the churches. The end of hard service comes soon. The beginning of all good things begins soon. He who has ears is blessed. Be ready. Be white. I come to the feast soon.

To all those who teach in seminaries and who are preachers, leaders, elders, and evangelists in churches, I command you to teach my words and only my words. Teach my truth in love and only my truth in love. No longer are you to call some of my truth "political", or "minutia", or brand some of my teaching as divisive, troublesome, politically incorrect, or offensive. If my words challenge you or trouble you, good; so they should. I am God and I have always challenged and troubled people. I love you. I don't leave you where you are at, but I grow you and I change lives. I do not change lives into something that is acceptable to churches and that lines up with your teachings. I change lives so that my children can increasingly resemble me. My Word is not your word and my ways are not your ways. Too much of what you do, say, think and practise is an offence to me. It should not be. It is not from me, never was from me, never will be from me. I am not an idol for you to shape with your hands. You are mine. I am the living God and I shape you with my hands. You will remove all YOUR teachings, all YOUR traditions, and all YOUR additions. You will put back and teach all my words that you have removed and that you have been failing to teach, and you will stop teaching in twisted ways that seek to explain that I didn't really mean what I said, as if you need to apologise to my children on my behalf.

It is a sad day when my children do not know where idolatry stops and where worship of me, the living God, begins. I command you to pray, fast, repent, and turn back to me and the purity of my Word, which you have mixed with sprinklings of idolatry. Humbly present yourself before my Holy Spirit for wise counsel and teaching, so that he can teach you more correctly, guide you into all truth, and teach you to teach all that I have taught.

FINDING THE TRUTH

Thursday, March 21, 2013

The way you do things, is it my way? You have traditional ways of accepting my truth, which renders it YOUR truth and not my truth. You have a clutter of practises and processes that are so buried within the fabric of YOUR churches—so deep down under the surface—that no longer is my truth truly seen or examined.

What is written is no longer all that is important. Instead, it is what your church believes, or you could put it this way: "I or we believe such and such." Doesn't that smell just a little scented with arrogance? When did it ever matter what you personally believe? Are you my god that I should listen to you now? Will you teach me my truth? Will you teach me how to believe more correctly? You might say, "Well God, you didn't exactly come down and explain to us what you meant, so we worked it out for ourselves, and you cannot blame us if we didn't get it right." Is that what I did? Would I be so stupid as to do that? Would I be so remiss in my care for you, to do that to you—to give you such a massive responsibility and permit such a high chance of getting it wrong, and then punish you and cheat you out of your salvation when you disappoint me and get it wrong?

Surprise, surprise, my children. I am not that god. I am your Father. I give good gifts. I did not leave you alone. I did not leave you with a book of my precious truth to muddle through and arrive at a big messy map of the way. All roads lead to where?

Let me remind you before I go on. My Scriptures are not a textbook and you are not at school or university. You do not face me and sit a test, and if you get 99% or 99.99% you have failed and cannot enter into my glory. How cruel and sick would I be if I did that? You would not give your children a test and, if they did not know everything perfectly, cast them out of your family to never see them again. Do not think that I am such a Father! I set the benchmark for being the very best and the most loving Father of all. There is no father more loving than I am. You have the best Father. The blood of my precious Son, his righteousness, redeems you and makes you precious and righteous children of mine.

Now that you have it clear that you are being addressed by your loving Father and I am addressing my much loved children, let's go back and look again at what you have been doing, for everything I have to say in this word to you is said in a spirit of correction, not a spirit of condemnation. I hold out my correction to you and you will be blessed if you take it up. Please show your love for me by walking closely with me, by listening to me, so that we may walk closer still, and so you may receive my full blessings in this life and in the next.

The fact is, my Son was not hinting when he said that I would send the Holy Spirit after he returned to his glory, but he stated it clearly. Among the roles that the Holy Spirit clearly fulfils for you are teaching you, guiding you into all my truth, and mentoring you along the way. As Jesus was to the disciples, so the Holy Spirit is to you, if, in fact, you are in Christ.

Turn off your televisions and your radios and computers; open your Bible and read. Pray and ask for the assistance of my Holy Spirit to know what my Word says. Speak constantly to my Holy Spirit, asking him to correct your thinking, and words, and actions so that everything about you will reflect my words.

There is no blessing in being wrong. There may be no punishment, no condemnation, but there is no blessing. You want to be right. I want you to be right because I want you to be fully nourished and nurtured by my truth. My Word is a blessing to you. It shows you the way. It shows you the yoke of your Rabbi Jesus. Jesus was gentle, compassionate, loving and forgiving. People loved him. Most churches have reinvented Jesus into one who is divisive, keen to reject, intolerant, and unkind. If someone does not go to a church you agree with, you treat them as a prospect to teach more correctly and, when they do not respond, you reject them as unworthy of your close friendship or as simply being annoying because they will not agree with everything you believe. This is not Jesus! You are not following your Rabbi when you conduct yourself in this way.

Remember, when you are angry with another, Jesus told you that we view that as akin to murder. There is much anger within and between Christians. You excuse it. You are being zealous for the truth. You are setting others straight. You are putting others in their place. Who made you judge, jury, and executioner? When you do this, you risk placing yourself on trial for murder. You are not condemned, neither should you condemn. I am not angry with you; neither should you be angry with others.

When you, as a sinner, try to sort out everyone's sins, you get yourself into more sin. You will say, but Paul did this and Paul did that, and some people were told to smarten up or get out of the church. The truth is that even my Son did nothing of himself, but he walked and talked with me, and did as I instructed him. So it was with Paul. What he said and did was correct, not because he did it, but because he was doing what I was telling him to do. Can't you see, if you imitate Paul or if you imitate Christ, the first thing you must do is be in touch with me—listen to me, listen to my Son, listen to my Holy Spirit. There are many things written in my Word. Do them and be blessed but, whenever you think you must correct, or advise, or assist someone else in their understanding or in their behaviour, ask us first.

Be humble. You have nothing but death to offer anyone else. Death is what you deserve. Death is where you belong. Be humble. The life that resides in you is not you and is not yours, but has been given to you. Nothing that you have that eternally profits another, is of you. Be humble and ask for our words, our advice, our assistance. We do not want you to act in your own strength for you have no strength. We want you to come humbly to us, admitting your faults and failures, your weaknesses and your lack of belief, and receive from us everything you need for life and godliness. Your life is given to you by us. You have no life to give others. We encourage you to take life from us and share it around to others.

This is why getting it right is important. My words have life and are life. Your words have death and are death. Add your words to my words and you give people partly death and partly life. This is not what we give to you or to anyone. Give the good gifts that we give to you and to others. Give our words and our truth. Our words are life and life abundant. Your words are death.

I do not say this to put you down. No matter how hard you try, you will make mistakes and you will get it wrong. We sympathise with your weaknesses. What we are saying in our correction is that we can help you. We want to help you. We have it right. If you want to get it right and have life to share with others, listen to us. We will give you the words to share, so that you may share life with others. If you will let us, we want to counsel you in how to read and understand our truth, how to glean nourishment from it, how to be strong in us, for our strength is your strength. We want to give you all a powerful stake in our kingdom. Our words and our ways are life—eternal life—and we want to give them to you so that you may share with others.

Right now, you are a muddle of life and death, white and black, glory and shame. You speak about a life of love and live a life of intolerance and anger. You want so much to get it right and to tell everyone else how to live, but your knowledge is contaminated and wrong. It is contorted out of shape and cannot fit the picture of Christ. The way you paint, live, and preach Scripture is a puzzle. It is a puzzle to you and to everyone.

Are the Jews right? No. Should they learn more correctly? Yes. Should they glorify Christ Jesus and trust in his salvation and look to him for their redemption? Yes. You cannot expect them to receive the thousands of messy, different, Christian church ideas and profit from them. Are the Catholics correct? No. Are the denominations right? No. Are there denominations in Christ Jesus? No. Did Jesus command you to go into all the world and teach 2,000 different doctrines? No. Are any of the exclusive churches that say they are the only churches that have it right really right? No. Are any of the Islamist ways of finding and worshipping God, correct? No. What of Mormonism, the Seventh-day Adventists, Jehovah's Witnesses or any other groups with special beginnings—are they correct? No. Is there some truth in all of them? Yes.

The fact is, Jesus said, 'Follow me'. Jesus told you that because I, his Father, gave him those words. Jesus' words were and are my words. In the same way that Jesus was listening to and sharing my words, so should you. Ask and you will receive, knock and you will have the door opened to you.

You are children with needs. We know that. We are the ones who have everything you need. We know that too. We want you to know that.

We want to give to you but few are hungry and thirsty, few are asking or knocking. Most are self-satisfied, most feel content and satisfied. Satisfied with what? Satisfied with their religion? Satisfied with their churches or their worship? You are worshippers of churches. You are worshipping religion. Your way of practising sets you apart and makes you unique. But this is not of God; this is not of Christ or my Holy Spirit. I would never give you something so empty, something so contrived, so man-made. Compared to what I have for you, you have little to nothing. You stand like starving children beside my sumptuously spread banquet table, angry and ready to fight with anyone who does not applaud your views. I don't applaud your views. Do you want to argue and fight with me too?

Saturday, April 27, 2013

I was reading the first 12 chapters of 1 Samuel and God showed me how similar his worldwide church was to God's people, Israel, in the days of Samuel. God called me from my reading and told me to write.

PEOPLE PLEASERS

As it was with Israel, I am God and redeemer of my Christian church; yet my church has usurped my Kingship. Am I not King? Did I not lift up my Son, Jesus the Christ, as King? Did I not say, "All authority has been given to him"? Then why is it that your first love is pleasing your creeds, your teachings of men? You will say, "We love your Word, oh God, and obey it. Tell us how we have loved our creeds more than you and your words." Let me tell you then, because I love you: You follow your traditions, your ceremonial customs, your ways that make your church. You are all different. You make your own preference and you are not comfortable with the preference of another. Does anyone of you care about my preference? You are men pleasers.

You want to be seen as a good Baptist or a good Catholic or a good Pentecostal or a good Anglican; but why? Because you want the respect, the acceptance, the pats on the back from all your friends. If you break ranks, you are seen as unfaithful to your church, or wavering, or as someone who cannot be relied upon, or as someone less than completely devoted and committed. Committed to what? Not to me, but to your church. Pleasing what? Not me, but your church, and your own ego and desire to be seen as legitimate, respectable, good, righteous, and Christian.

My loved children, can you not see the harm in this? Can you not see the foothold you have given to Satan? What happens deep in your heart? You have a divided heart; that is what happens. You cannot be fully for me because you are partly for your church and your friends. You do not want to offend them but you will offend me. You will say, "But we do not offend you as Christians loyal to our church?" It is true that you have become so familiar and comfortable with your ways and your thinking that you cannot see the offence it is to me, and you cannot see the harm and the danger it is to you. You were born into it. The whole world of Christians sees nothing wrong with adding, taking away, modifying, shaping and interpreting my Word the way they want to. And as long as they leave Christ in, they think it is okay. It is not okay. Can't you see what all your different churches have done and are doing? The moment you meet to choose a pattern, a ceremonial way, a method, you are making choices for me and for my Son, the Christ. The moment you meet to make decisions about your form of assembly, and worship, and belief, you are making decisions for me and for my Son, the Christ. This is not right. This has never been right, my children.

I have a kingdom. I am King. I decide. You are my ambassadors. You march under my flag, not your flag. Mine is not a kingdom that is divided. Mine is not many nations. Mine is one kingdom, one people, under one flag. You have hoisted the flags of your different churches, separated and divided by your different creeds and beliefs. Yes, you are my children. Yes, you are saved by the blood of my Son, and this is why I write to you at the end of the end times. I call you back to be one again, as it was in the first century.

Can't you see? The devil is one! The enemy and all his demons are united. The world is at war. It is the greatest battle of all time. It is a battle waged by spiritual forces and powers. Yet it has a physical element, with Christians on one side and evil people on the other; those standing with me, trying to live moral lives and seeking to spread the message of the gospel of Christ, and those bent on increasing temptation, sin, and distress.

There is one sword. It is my sword of truth. But you have blunted my sword by living, preaching, and choosing your churches as if there were many truths, picking the one you like best. This is a blunt and laughable truth. There is either truth or there is not. There is no blunt truth. My Word, my Scriptures are the truth. Open them, examine them again, get rid of your ideas that you think are best, and accept what is from me and only from me, for my words have power; your words have none. Worse still, by adding your powerless words, you weaken my words and you dilute my truth.

Lucifer is strong and all those with him, knowingly or unwittingly, are with him and stand like one man. Their task is easy compared to mine. They can pick and choose anything, anyway that is not mine. They can take anything that is not my truth. They can do anything except take my one truth to believe it and act upon it, to worship and glorify me and my Son, and to live according to my ways. But it is not so for me or for my children. There is only one truth. There is only one way. There is only Christ. Yes, he forgives you for failure but can you fail less? Your churches present to the world many truths, many ways, and many Christs. You have Lucifer laughing as if he never expected his job would be made so easy by the very followers of Christ. Lucifer has plans to tempt this world. Many will be fooled— even many who presently cannot see the truth from variations of the truth.

Did I ever ask you to do something impossible? Yes, you are weak. I am strong. I know it is impossible for you to know the way. I know that the New Testament, as you call it, weaves about and is a scattered mishmash of thoughts and principles. Many of you will be thinking, "Well, what did you expect, oh God? You gave us letters and histories that can come up with lots of conclusions because they are so often non-specific." What did I expect? I didn't expect you to come to your own conclusions. I didn't expect you to establish churches and schools of thought based upon your own conclusions about what I was possibly saying, perhaps suggesting, or maybe meaning.

FIRST CENTURY CHURCH

Please think back to how it was done and intended to be done. Christ led his disciples and his apostles. He taught them. When Christ left this earth physically, he told his followers to wait for the Holy Spirit. The Holy Spirit guides into all truth. The Holy Spirit corrects. The Holy Spirit is your mentor, your counsellor; the one who shows you the way, teaches you the meaning, and gives you the method. If you cannot hear clearly from the Holy Spirit, sit down and stop leading, because all you are good at in leadership is giving Satan a foothold and making a big mess. My Holy Spirit is key. Listen to him.

In the first century, the teaching, the correction, the worship, the conversions, the growing, the churches, the leadership, the kingdom were all under the direction of the Holy Spirit. Was everything and everyone perfect? No. Was every church correct and doing everything correctly? No. However, they did have men who planted the churches in Christ's name, as Christ's servants. Those leaders within the kingdom were of one mind because they were all directed from one mind—that being mine. There is nothing more obvious on earth today, in the Christian churches, than the influence of church leadership that is not led personally by me. Leaders are not hearing personally from me. Churches and church leadership are all over the place. It is a spiritual mess. It is all so confusing and mixed up because it is under the direction of the confused and the mixed up.

Please believe me when I say that I am not surprised or disappointed in you being confused and mixed up. You should be. What do you know? You are my little ones. The best you can do is bumble along. When it comes to spiritual things, you are as bright as being in a dark room, groping around looking for the light switch so you can turn on the light and see. I am the power, the lighting, and the switch. I am the one who tells you what you are seeing, describes the benefit of what you are seeing, and shows you how to change your life and your world by using all I have given you to use. On your own, when it comes to spiritual things, you are blind. You are lone, blind men climbing Mount Everest and expecting to find your way to the victory of ascending the summit. There is no way. You do not have a way. Jesus Christ is the Way. He is the only one who knows the way and can show you the way.

I know many will say, "But you gave us the Word and with the New Testament, we know the way." Oh yeah? Look around you. Can you see THE WAY or is there a blurred, wobbly, wavering thing that you have set up and tried to call a path? I don't want to knock you or ridicule your efforts because I know how many of you are sincere, but the devil is also sincere and when he commands his soldiers to jump, they say, "How high?" The churches are under so many commanders all calling out slightly different commands to the army of God, so that no one is able to hear any message clearly. Everyone is saying what's important and it is all a bit different; everyone can take their pick as to who they listen to more at any one time.

Can't you see what you have done to me and to my command? My kingdom must have one voice and one commander. There must be one chief officer to whom all eyes look and to whom all ears listen. Presently there are thousands upon thousands, all bumbling about trying to pretend they know the way. From time to time, I have sent reformers. You know that. It made a difference, but the job of reforming never stops; the task of listening to me and following me never stops.

Lucifer is working on a plan to deceive the world and, if possible, to deceive all believers. I do not want you to be deceived. His plan was proposed thousands of years ago. Don't think of vagaries because the devil does not have a vague plan. You, in the last days of the last days, must be prepared for what is to come. Your protection is me. I am the Way. You must listen to me or follow leadership that is listening to me. I bring blessings; without me there are no blessings—only curses. Get close to me. Walk and talk with me. Love me from the heart.

Fall in love with me and become one with me. Together we can do so much. Alone, you can do nothing, except make a mess. If all the churches, all the leadership, all the saints were together as one with me, you cannot imagine the difference this would make to my kingdom and the difference this would make to your joy! Please listen to me. Be brave; cast off what you call church and come back to listening only to your God and Saviour and King! Let us examine my Scriptures together. Let me guide you into all truth. But first, let's get used to walking and talking together. This is not about getting the right feeling. Feelings can trick you because the devil can deceive through feelings. This is about my thoughts being your thoughts. This is about you having the mind of Christ. This is about me in your head—instructing, correcting and leading you personally, and about you always being able to test me by asking me to declare Jesus as God and, in so doing, testing the one who is instructing you. Let's take this journey together, the journey of the first century. Let's recreate the church of the first century which had words and power, and which was one with me—God. Let's bring back at the end, that which was in the beginning—one person at a time! A full connection to Jesus, the vine—not some weak and distant version of Jesus. I will see you bear much fruit and you will love that; and so will I.

PRIORITIES

Thursday, May 16, 2013

I want to draw a distinction between the church and the works of the church in the kingdom, David. Too many churches are fat cows concerned with appearance. The adornment I seek is not to the church building, but spiritual adornment in the hearts and attitudes of my children who love me—who are in love with me—and who are eagerly awaiting the return of their Bridegroom. Instead, all too often, it is the organ, or the stairs, or the baptistery, or lights, props, seats, etc. which look so beautiful, while the leaders and so many of the people look impoverished. I don't expect your buildings and facilities to be uncomfortable or substandard. But why should they be 5 star? Unless you desire to pose and say to those around you, "look at what I have. Look at where I worship. I worship at a real church, a beautiful church, a church that looks luxurious, a church where there is a long waiting list for weddings, a church that people want to photograph and be photographed in." Worship is not a show for passers-by; nor are my buildings of worship. Make your hearts a show of humility and all the qualities of my Son. Don't make your buildings the show. In saying this, I do not require that the mistakes of the past—when physical opulence was equated to spiritual opulence—be destroyed. Do not tear down the physical mistakes of the past but change the way you view them and the way you use them. Is it me you worship or your mighty buildings? If it is your buildings, your worship is clearly in vain and your heart in peril.

So, beware that your church budgets, your expenditures, your financial priorities reflect your spiritual priorities. Are most of your expenditures going into my kingdom—into glorifying me, into relieving suffering while sharing the good news that salvation is free, and causing many to be filled with joy and praises for me? Or is most of your budget dedicated to wages, building payments, or maintenance? Are the financial scraps going to the hungry, the suffering, and the hungry for good news? Is 90% for you and 10% for me? You ask my children to tithe; then you take their 10% gift and, after you have spent all you can on yourselves, on your bureaucracy and administration, you give me 10% to run my great kingdom on. How very stingy of you. It is no wonder that my children are not inclined to give 10%, let alone far more. What if the church reversed its budget and ensured that 90% of the gifts of my children went into evangelism, into relief of suffering, into my kingdom? How much more reason would my children have to give, as they witnessed the world turned upside down for praise and worship of me.

I am not talking about the many tiny churches that struggle, where only 30 or 50 of my children may worship. But of these many small churches, couldn't four or five—or better still, five or ten—churches join together and reduce employment and building costs through efficiency of numbers? If you are listening to my Holy Spirit and obeying him, that is what you will do. And why so many buildings? Does a tiny group need a building? For that matter, does a group of 1,000 or more require a building? What for, if it is only for a few hours of worship and praise? What a crazy, gluttonous waste. It is no wonder that so little gets done in my kingdom, when so much emphasis is placed on my children getting a building to worship in, like a young family wanting a house to live in. You already have houses to live in. Would you buy a house to live in it for two hours each week? Would a business survive if it bought premises and only used them two hours each week? Why not rent premises until your churches reach 10,000 or 15,000 worshippers? There are great facilities to rent with space available. If you are a community church in a poor area and your church is a safe house for the vulnerable, and your building is full every day of the week, feeding the poor, caring for the sick, protecting the weak, and counselling the sad, that is different. You need a building. But even then, only buy if it is much more economical than renting.

Stop sitting on and sitting in your money, your pews, and your buildings, but pour the giving into my kingdom. My church should be a financial fountain, not a stopped up financial reservoir—not a fat cow. Get lean, get fit, get mobile and work in my kingdom efficiently, making a lot happen with a little, instead of getting so little done with a lot.

CHURCH IN THE MARKETPLACE

Wednesday, May 29, 2013

Why is it that churches have so limited a view on raising money to assist the poor, the hungry, the orphans, the widows, and getting evangelists into the kingdom to preach salvation through Christ? You establish hospitals, schools, and counselling centres—usually with a lot of government tax money—and this is good and productive. But why have you limited yourself to this? Why does there seem to be something that stops you from using the savvy of the world to take full, moral and honest advantage of the natural, extended-family attributes of the church, in order to establish profit-making businesses of which my kingdom is the first beneficiary. Churches keep pushing members to give more and more, and encouragement in generosity is great, but why should the burden of the heavy financial lifting weigh down individual members of the church?

Imagine, for a moment, that the church not only encourages members to establish businesses, but that the church boldly establishes businesses. These would be businesses that are a shining example of Christ and the qualities of the Holy Spirit in action, where employees are treated with dignity and encouraged to take time to pray, to read Scripture, and to discuss that which is spiritually edifying and nourishing for the soul. What if these same businesses employed a balanced strategy of half its employees being Christian believers and the other half non-believers? Imagine the quality of living benefits if employees could have health care and mortgages looked after by these firms so that Christians could avoid the burden of crippling interest and could, instead, give far more generously to my kingdom via the church. The way you do it today creates so much waste, stress, and guilt on the part of my children—guilt and stress over not being able to give as generously as they would like. Church businesses could support employees and release them from labour for short-term mission trips, and fund training and support for employees who want to respond to my call for them to go into my mission fields full-time. If churches are small, they could amalgamate, join forces, and pool resources to establish new firms, invest in existing firms, or buy successful established firms.

Yes, the world will be furious at you for getting smart with money, like the world is; but do it with a heart for your workers and with a heart for my kingdom. Lucifer will be furious that the church awoke financially to the opportunities I laid before it. Are there huge spiritual challenges in all this? Obviously, yes! You will have to be honest, like I am honest. You will have to pray for my power and my blessing, and you will have to follow my lead, for I will head up your firms. You will consult the Holy Spirit in all things, listen to him, and do what he tells you to do. In other words, your church firms will be places that are deeply spiritual from top to bottom. You will have to be kind and fair, and show love and the qualities of my Holy Spirit in all areas of your conduct—behind closed doors with your employees and when you are on show. Your firms will be centres for spiritual enrichment. Your business leaders and your CEOs will be spiritual leaders, spiritual CEOs—not just be good at business in a way that stinks of tolerated sin. There would be no abuse, no arguing, no anger, no undermining, no gossip, no lusting, but a lot of prayer, lots of building up and encouragement. Most of all, these firms would be fine spiritual examples which exhibit faith and trust that I know what I am doing, and that you must consult me, listen to me, and do what I say.

This will not be like doing church. It will not be like suffering each other through gritted teeth and frozen grins for one or two hours a week, and feeling like you have done your Christian duty to love your enemies. No, you will work alongside your brothers and sisters constructively, and love them, and be considerate of them. There will be nowhere to park your Christianity, nowhere to hide it. You will, instead, be living your faith every day. I know of hospitals that are supposedly run by Christians—by churches—and they are filled with anger, strife, jealousy, envy, hate, and abuse. Do better. Learn self-control. Take my virtues seriously. How can you claim to love me when you do not love your brothers and sisters?

DO NOT JUDGE

I see more of you going to the effort of setting up websites filled with judgement and condemnation for your brothers and sisters. If anyone thinks or believes something that is the tiniest bit different from your belief, you put them on your going-to-hell list. When did you sit down and ask me if I wanted you to do that? These are my sons and daughters you are condemning. Doesn't it make you feel concerned that, amongst your list for hell, are some I call close friends, and I wish you were as close to me as they are. You excuse yourself, looking into my Scriptures, plucking out verses to justify your hate and loathing for your brothers and sisters. Beware! Look at where you stand and how you walk. I love you, but do not turn my love and favour into an opportunity to hold a hate festival. Let me make it clear that, when you insult them, you insult me; and when you judge and condemn them, you judge and condemn me. They are my children and I am their Father. Is my arm too short to correct them? I do, but I do it in love and patience. Those you accuse are changing and growing, but are you? These children of mine are not hate-filled—they are not persecuting and defaming you. They lift up my Son and encourage others to set their hope and trust in him and fall in love with him. None are perfect; all are flawed. All need transformation and are in need of change and growth. And this is happening.

Instead of trying to carve up my children—your brothers and sisters—like a spit roast, why don't you try bringing my children together in peace and warmth as your family? Try honestly sharing your weaknesses and your strengths together, and blessing each other, for you are all broken and all are failures. All of you, if you seek healing and victory, will find what you desire in my Son and in me—not in yourself. Stop setting yourselves up as judges and executioners because I do not do that to you, nor to those you accuse, despise, and reject. Remember, Satan is bringing accusation again you and against all my children all the time. Don't be like Satan; be like me. If you do not stand, you risk setting yourself up to a standard and measure of judgement that is your own. I love you so very much. You are breaking my heart. If only you would stop and come into my arms for my love and forgiveness. Yet I fear you will, instead, choose to also put my servant, my scribe, on your list for condemnation and judgement. In doing so, you are writing your own name on your list and no one else's, for you are not the judge. When you are filled with my Spirit and judge righteously and with love, then, and only then, can you judge. But then you will be a very different judge—one who does not want to judge, but wants to understand, sympathise, and strengthen. Be wise and take heed of my warning so that you do not perish on your own executioner's sword.

ISLAMIC CHILDREN

To my children who adhere to Islam—those with sincere hearts filled with love for me—I am God, and the name "Allah" is simply the Arabic word for "God"; so you are certainly worshippers of me, the living God. But you do not understand Christ, and you have not accepted him, and you do not understand his sacrifice for your sins. There is only one God and that is me. This is truth. But if I choose to enter into bodily form, walk this earth, teach followers to spread my very good news, and die for the sins of the whole world, is this not a good gift that I give to you and to everyone—forgiveness of your sins and eternal life?

You are troubled that God cannot have a Son. With my qualities, being God, being divine, how would you like me to explain myself to you so that you may understand me? I chose the simplest and easiest way for sincere people to understand, but you still find me impossible to understand as "Christ". I sympathise, for I know I am not easy to get your head around. But let me ask you this: Is it too difficult for me, who has the ability to be everywhere at once—individually, personally, and generally—and who knows all things, and who is infinite in power, and eternally enthroned in heaven, to be on earth in physical form as "Christ", and to have my Holy Spirit guide all my children in the truth, mentoring them in the best way to live? Is that too difficult for me? If you think that this is something that is too difficult for any man or woman to understand, then what would you suggest?

Should I have called myself "God in heaven", "God on earth", and "God inside the hearts of my believers"? Would that have confused you and had you counting up three Gods, and arguing over which God was the real God, the biggest God, the most powerful God? No matter how you put it or what you call me, I am God. I am difficult to understand and I will always be difficult to understand. My angels prefer to marvel, love me, and be amazed at my works and achievements, rather than try to understand me.

The simplest explanation that I have for you is that if I were to die for the sins of mankind—and there is no other way to redeem any man of sins—I would have to die and offer up my spiritually perfect life, but it would still have to be a physical life that could be literally sacrificed. Nevertheless, while on earth in the flesh, in the form of Jesus, I also had to be outside the flesh in order to have the power to do the works that would show the Christ to be not just any man. Christ, the man, also had to demonstrate what it is to relate to Father God and draw strength and guidance from him. In the form of the Father, I was enthroned in heaven so my children could pray to me. In the form of the Holy Spirit, I was working with my divine power during the earthly life of Christ and I do so to this day. If there is a simpler way to do what I did, perhaps you would be so kind as to advise me. Whether I call myself "I" or "we" should not disturb you. Please excuse me if I say that it doesn't take much to challenge you!

You need to sit, ask me, listen to me, and do what I say. I will never tell you that Christ was just a prophet who lived and died like all the others, because I cannot dishonour myself. I will never tell you that you do not need faith in Christ to receive forgiveness for your sins. I will also never offer you a paradise where I am not, for I am the Father of all people. All people are my children, whether they are children who love me or who do not love me. Those of you who have sincere hearts are being visited by Christ—the one in white. You have heard. You know that many leaders in your communities are being visited. When they are honest and share what I have to say, they are shunned and dishonoured.

Do I have to visit all of you to convince you of the truth about Christ? I am also visiting ordinary Islamic believers to spread the word about the truth of Christ. It is much as it was in the days of my son Saul or Paul. He too needed a visit to be convinced of Christ, but he was sincere. However, most of his colleagues were not sincere and immediately set about persecuting him. Why didn't they ask me if his report about his visit from Christ was genuine? Why don't you ask me if the reports by your leaders about being visited by Christ are true?

Regarding methods of worship, there is no strict form. My children, within reason, should feel free to honour me with worship from their hearts, in manners meaningful to them, without others judging one form of worship better or worse, acceptable or not acceptable, sinful or holy. If you are coming before me with a sincere heart and pure motives, and seek to worship me in spirit and in truth, whether you are wearing suits, grass skirts, or T-shirts and shorts is of little consequence. I know your heart. I see your heart. Purify your heart and don't come before me with love on your lips for me, and hate in your hearts for your fellow man—believer or unbeliever. Don't be deceived; I am well aware of the filth, immorality and injustice being done in the name of Christianity, Islam, and Judaism. Such iniquity does not come from me, nor from those who seek me with a sincere heart and those who seek to be holy.

JEWISH CHILDREN

To the Jews I say, why did you miss the Christ? Were your own prophets not good enough for you? Why do others believe the promised Christ, but not you? Yes, you are my children; you are Abraham's children, but in what is your faith invested? Is it in me, or in wealth and in your history? Set an example of love in your region—of tolerance and kindness—for love, justice, and mercy are very important to me and cruel persecution of near neighbours does not honour me. I sent Christ to you! Your people did not honour me but hated, despised and killed me. I am God, so I knew what you would do to me. But now I call you to repent and honour me by honouring Christ. You know you have heard that many Jews, high and low, are being visited by Christ—the man in white. Yet you continue to reject me. You reject those who share their encounters with you and you close your heart to my message. You know from the prophets when the Christ had to come. You understand that the Christ was God. Yet, in not believing the Christ today, what are you really saying you believe? Do you believe the prophets were wrong, or that they were liars? Do you believe Christ was wrong, or that he was a liar? Whatever the answer is, you know better than Christians what the prophets wrote about the Messiah; and if he did not come, that makes me the liar, for they were my prophets. I am the Messiah.

Search your heart, search the Scriptures, and be honest. You fear the rejection of your people, your families and your communities. So instead, you reject the Messiah. And most of you band together to persecute any of your own who will believe the truth that your prophets spoke. Read what Jesus Christ taught while he walked this earth and ask your God if it is true. Listen to me, learn from me, believe, and change.

A very similar persecution awaits any adherents to Islam who believe in Christ, and this is a hindrance to me and the blessings I have for you, now and eternally. Stop hating and persecuting, and start loving and believing, because I am the God of love, not hate! Ask me and listen to me. Am I not God? Can I not communicate perfectly and easily with you? Should you not make welcome my thoughts—the thoughts of your God—into your heart and into your head, for your blessing and guidance? I love you so much, my dear children. But many of you do not know me. You do not know my love for you. You do not know my heart for you and you do not understand that I long for closeness with you. Please, I want to establish my tabernacle inside you and make my home in your heart to be one with you forever—if you would only want me!

THREE IN ONE

Thursday, May 30, 2013

Why should I need to try to explain myself, as if I should present myself before you for examination? Yet I will, in the hope that you may someday be satisfied and simply choose to love me? Why am I one God, yet appear to be three? The simple fact is that there is a difference between form and function, just as you can make the same distinction about yourself. Although you have many giftings—there are many things you are poorer at or better at—yet you are still one man or one woman. When you think, you talk to yourself and reason with yourself as if you were not alone, not one person; yet you are. Multiple thinking and multiple gifting do not make you more than one individual; it simply indicates that you are made in my image. I am one, yet I function as three. There is balance and strength in three. It also means that I can empty myself, become a little lower than the angels, live in the flesh, but still be deity, reign in heaven over all mankind, over all the unseen spiritual world, and over the universe. How could I come as God and not as a man? The body of a man can die, but I, God, cannot die. Does it offend you that I died for you, that I sacrificed myself for you, that I suffered and died for you?

You Jews are so spiritual; your knowledge is great. Where did your rabbis get their spiritual knowledge, discernment, and insights if not from me personally? But you do not want to know about, believe and glorify Christ. Haven't you noticed that you do not sacrifice anymore? And why not? Because sacrifices are offered by your priests and you no longer know who is qualified by tribe to be a priest. So where are your sin sacrifices? Where is your redemption? Will your many prayers and devout moral living rid you of your sins? I say, no! Where is my Holy of Holies and where is my Ark of the Covenant? Where is your God? Did he leave you? Did he break his promises to Abraham and to you? No, the Messiah came, but you rejected him. You reject him to this day and you choose to live with no inner peace and intimacy with me.

My prophets, told the truth; so why do you live a lie? Why do you refuse to look at what my prophets foretold of the Christ and when he would come? Why will you not repent in sackcloth and ashes and come before me as my humble children and accept your salvation— your redemption in the Messiah? What salvation, what redemption do you cling to? Your stubbornness? Christ came to your fathers and they rejected him. Now, like your fathers, you reject him. You reject your salvation. You reject the Messiah. You reject me. You reject us. Am I not good enough for you? If it is not sufficiently obvious to you—in case you are so blind and brainwashed by your leaders who are not prophets and not priests—you live with your guilt and your fear every day. Abraham was a wonderful son, but he could not save you from your sins. Moses was a great friend and son, but your hope of redemption was not found in him. You Jews all know that the Messiah is your hope—your only hope. If you will listen to me, let me bless you. Listen to me, read the words of your Messiah and ask me if it is not the truth. As I promised Abraham, multitudes have believed and accepted Christ and look to him for their salvation, but not my children of Abraham. Yet a few of you listened and, in the Messiah, have made peace with me. My children, please listen. Time is short. Be wise and listen to me.

Christians, Jews, and Islamists, please accept the free gift of forgiveness of your sins offered by the Messiah. Set your hope in him. Be baptised into the Messiah and rise to new spiritual life beginning now, and for all eternity, with your heart in mine and my heart in yours, so that you and I may be one, as the Father, the Son and the Spirit are one. Become one in Christ. Live for me and bring me glory through your unity under Christ. We are not divided but one God. As it is with us, so it is with you. You are more than one person but you are one people under Christ—one unified spiritual race under one God, bringing me glory in my kingdom.

Do you not know that Satan, Lucifer, and all who look to him, are one? Evil is unified, while my children fight, and argue, and despise each other. How can an army have victory when they march under so many different leaders, when they refuse to cooperate with each other, when they will not work together, sacrifice together, grow together, share together, and bring me glory and share in my victory together? Christ has triumphed and is victorious, but in his kingdom, his children must reign in unity. Lift up his name with one voice and work for righteousness and against evil, under the authority and power of Jesus Christ.

When the Messiah walked this earth, he told you many things. The words he spoke were not his words, but my words. I spoke into his thoughts and he spoke my words out of his mouth. His friends—those who believed him to be the Messiah—under the guidance of the Holy Spirit, wrote the Messiah's words. Read the Messiah's words! The Messiah is the Way and his are the words of life. Listen to him!

CHRISTIAN CHILDREN

My Christian churches have presented themselves so arrogantly, with positions and stances that are superior and exclusive. In effect, they say, we are the way—the only way—our words are the words that give life. At the very same time, they are very poor at humbling themselves before me, before the Messiah, to ask for wisdom, knowledge, and understanding from the Holy Spirit, and to listen and do as the Messiah did. Christian churches, you have lifted yourselves up; you have become your own authority—your own Christ. You are a bad example of Christ. You should be listening and receiving teaching, counsel, and training. But instead, you are too busy teaching things you do not know or understand and cannot live. Christ is Christ; not you, not your churches, not your leaders. You speak in your name as if salvation, and power, and divine authority resided with you. Who are you people who do little but defame me?

The Messiah spoke my simple words. Before he left you, he made clear that the Holy Spirit would lead, guide, and direct you into all truth. Have you become too good for the Holy Spirit? Have you become too smart? You now lead yourselves, you now direct yourselves, and you now speak your own truth. Where has your leadership led? What path have you taken and where has it taken you? To division and endless, meaningless squabbling over what is written, intended and meant. You were not left alone to do this, but you have left yourselves alone to do this. Humble yourselves, cry out to me, listen to the Holy Spirit, ask him where you have gone wrong, ask him what you must change and do to get it right. Listen to him. I have not left you alone to fight over a small book that contains spiritual mysteries above and beyond your abilities to grasp and understand on your own. Or are you smarter and more spiritual than the Messiah? The Messiah had the prophets and the Scriptures, but he did not trust himself to his own understanding and knowledge.

If I, the Holy Spirit, guide you into all truth, how good will your truth be? Far better than what you call truth. When I offer myself to be your closest friend, mentor, and lover of your soul, why would you turn to yourself to find the way to your salvation, and speak into yourself words of life? Surely you have experienced enough spiritually from me to know that my Word is not just words on a page—not just a book. The Messiah, as he spoke to crowds, told them plainly that they could not understand my words unless understanding and meaning was given from above. As it was for the Messiah, so it was for the Jewish crowds, and so it is for you.

All of you who call yourself Christian, whether Catholic, Protestant, Church of Latter Day Saints, etc., you all have the same problem. You have all found your own different way. You have all listened too much to man and too little to the Holy Spirit. In Christ, there is salvation, but in the words and interpretations of man, there is none. You have faith in Christ but Christ speaks, as promised, through the Holy Spirit. Listen to him as he unpacks for you his words of life and leads you along his way to salvation. The Messiah died to give you life that is abundant, so that you may thrive in peace and have power that can only come from an intimate relationship with me; not puzzling and bickering over words on a page.

I hear accusations and judgements against the Roman Catholic Church. It is as if they were not Christians, as if they were not my children, and your brothers and sisters. Here is a question for you: "Which church was it that I entrusted with the canonisation of my Word?" It was the Roman Catholic Church that I entrusted this important work to. Few of my children from Protestant churches disagree that the Scriptures they now call the Old Testament and the

New Testaments are my Word. Was I at work ensuring the quality of my Word? Definitely! The Holy Spirit worked in the lives of sons entrusted with this work and they worked as they were moved, and as they were instructed. Were they perfect sons? No. Were they going to a perfect church? No. Nevertheless, they were beloved sons who were close to me!

And what of the calling that I made clear to Mother Teresa? Did I call her to lift up the Catholic Church? No. I called her to love as Jesus loves, to be an example of the love of Jesus to the world, and to thereby lift up Christ. I called her to work for me and she said, "Yes." I would rather use imperfect people who will say yes and go into the work I give them, than theoreticians who want to ponder the ins and the outs of perfection and how close they and others are. How can I call perfect sons and daughters when there are none? How can I call sons and daughters who go to the perfect church? There is no perfect church. Christ is perfect and his righteousness makes my children perfect and fit to enter my service on earth, and my home in heaven. Christ makes the church perfect. But all my children are faulty, weak, and imperfect people, whose only way of being perfect is found in the perfection of the Messiah, and whose only power to live right and please me is found in the power of the Holy Spirit.

Common to Catholic thinking is that they are the only true church. Who told you that? You did not hear that from the Holy Spirit. Is salvation in the Catholic Church? No! Salvation is in Christ Jesus. Lift up the name of Jesus and not your name.

It amazes me what a muddle my Christian children have made of the way to enter into my salvation. It is as if each of you have chosen one aspect and made it all there is. Where is the sinner's prayer in my Word? Yes, there is a point at which a good heart is convicted, remorseful, and wants salvation, but why turn it into a ritual, when it is a deeply personal interaction between me and my offspring who want to come into my arms and call me Father and Saviour.

Do you want to displace me—to take me out of the picture from moment one—to distract the little ones with your words? Do you not trust me to be at work deep within them, where you cannot see? So, out of your doubt and lack of trust in me, you want to know what the new believer is doing and saying by having them say it out loud? Would it not be best to introduce them to me—to awaken their minds to the opportunity that I want to talk with them and to guide them personally from moment one?

Stop establishing your rituals. It kills spontaneity, the uniqueness of the individual, and the personal way in which the Messiah, the Holy Spirit and I, Father God, want to connect with our new child. Teach them all I say about salvation—all that the Messiah, his apostles, and his evangelists taught from the Holy Spirit. I do not want you all doing everything the way your church does it. It's not your church; it is my church. Do it my way. If you do not know what to do, ask me. But it is also written; so, take an interest and read it.

There are many examples of the process through which new believers come into me and into the church. Don't make it up. Don't do it your way or your church's way. But do it my way, the Holy Spirits way! Any other way shows your arrogance, is divisive, and is in opposition to unity in us. And remember that, just like a new physical birth, it is only the spiritual beginning and one must grow into me. Spiritual growth occurs over a lifetime and is nurtured by brothers and sisters—a spiritual family that is being led, and guided, and nurtured by me. May you never forget that it is Christ's righteousness that is given to you as your righteousness so that you can enter into close union with me as you approach the throne of righteousness with confidence.

PERFECTIONISM

Presently, some churches follow a one-step plan while others have a five-step plan. Then there are those who must see blood in the water or baptism is not considered to be effective. And still others include speaking in a foreign language as a necessary proof that a person is saved. If your church has been around for 1,000 years, will you believe what it teaches? If your preacher or priest is trained, qualified, and ordained, will you believe what he teaches? Other churches declare that they are the only correct church, so salvation is only recognised by God if you attend a church with their name on the front of it. Is it important to do what I say in my Word? Yes, very important! Is it important to get everything perfectly correct and do everything perfectly, as it is written in my Word? Yes, absolutely; it is very important. If you get anything wrong in my Scriptures and you are not perfectly correct in everything you know and do, will I still call you son or daughter and save you? Yes, I will.

Think about this for a moment. What sort of God would I be, if you had to get my Word perfectly right and live a perfect life? The sort of God I would be then is not the sort of God who loves you so much that he would die for you! I do demand perfection but I know you can never be perfect. And that is why the Messiah came, lived the perfect life that only God in the flesh can, and died as the sacrifice for your sins, taking upon himself your sins and placing upon you his righteousness. If I insisted that you get my Word perfectly correct, why did I write the biographical accounts, the histories, and the letters to the churches and church workers in such an imperfect, rather muddled, and confusing way? Was it because I wanted to condemn you? The

Messiah could have avoided sacrificing himself if your condemnation was all I was interested in.

Why are our, at times, almost anecdotal and often simple recounts of events so far from a black and white law code? Because the Holy Spirit guides you into all truth, gives you knowledge, and teaches you how to apply my truth to your life. Therefore there can be variation in what is taught by the Holy Spirit, because he will not teach what you are not ready to know. The Holy Spirit is patient and kind. He knows where you are in your growth and doesn't want to get too far ahead of you to cause you to despair and give up. This is part of the reason why the church has more mature members leading—those who have learned more from the Holy Spirit over a longer time. Nevertheless, it is important that such leaders be patient, knowing that pleasing me is not about perfection, but about the desire to love me and the desire to grow and become more like me. If it were any other way, none of you would have a relationship with me now or eternally, and the Messiah's death would have been in vain.

We are like Fathers with very small children. We know you cannot read and understand as we do, that you make many mistakes, lack self-control, and fail to please in many ways. But if you love us and desire to grow to be more like us, then we are pleased. We can be pleased because the Messiah has paid the price for all your imperfections. However, even though you are so imperfect and we approach you with such loving kindness, you approach the imperfection in others with intolerance, impatience, ridicule, and condemnation. Extend to others the kindness we extend to you. Or do you want us to treat you as you treat others?

Approach me humbly, seek the counsel of the Holy Spirit, and learn from me. I am one and I have one church. Be my one church. Cooperate with the Holy Spirit. Love me. Love one another.

I enjoy the company of a child with a contrite heart far more than a heart arrogantly confident that they have got it all correct. To know me and to be honest with me about your sins and weaknesses—to know how greatly you are loved by me and are forgiven of all your filth, and sin, and weakness—is the beginning point of a potentially great and close relationship with me. You cannot stand confidently before me and my purity, while bragging about how good you are—how much better you are than your brothers and sisters—as if you believed you were saved by how worthy you are. I love you and the Holy Spirit is always with you to assist you to change to be more like me. Listen to me, and if you cannot listen to me, then listen to people who are listening to me.

DECEPTION

To churches that worship me as God, but who find ways to diminish Christ's divine equality, I say beware. Anything opposed to Christ is not from me. The devil will use my Word increasingly to try to "prove" that I am bad—that Christ is weak. Worshippers of Lucifer are taught by demons to pervert all the words of my prophets into lifting up Lucifer as saviour and as god to be worshipped. The Holy Spirit will not teach you that, but will, instead, guide you into truth that gives relationship with me and life eternal. Lucifer teaches his worshippers that in the garden of Eden, I held Adam and Eve as captives and would not give them the full blessings to grow and become like me, like God. Lucifer perverts what happened in the garden to where he is viewed as the saviour who rescued Adam and Eve from a bad God, and who freed them and taught them to become just like God. Therefore, take care, because for thousands of years, Lucifer has been preparing to teach the world how bad I am and how good he is. He is parading as the God of love. Do not be deceived as many soon will be. Do not diminish the Messiah. Do not diminish your Saviour, Lord, and God, for diminishing God elevates Lucifer. See, I have warned you. You can trust the Holy Spirit. Do not trust anyone who speaks to you anything that is not endorsed by the Holy Spirit, and do not trust anyone who argues against my black and white, clear and obvious Word.

Angels who allied with Lucifer and went to war against me will perform great signs and amazing wonders to capture your attention, to impress you, and to cause you to want to believe them and obey them. They will teach all the people of the world to worship Lucifer as god. They are liars; and every word they speak is a lie, everything they do is a lie, and everything they plan is a lie. Do not believe anything that comes from them. This is a great end-times delusion that is soon to come. See, I have warned you in love. I have told you in advance so that you will not be deceived. There will be a great struggle on earth between good and evil. Choose the good, choose life! The Holy Spirit is the only sure way for you to stay in, and be confident in, the truth. Close to your God, to me, is the only place you want to be. Read my Word and know it correctly for it will protect you from the great delusion soon to come upon the earth.

DRAW NEAR

Draw close to me; become one with me. Lift up Messiah as Saviour God. Worship under one worldwide banner, Christ. I am about to come upon the earth with greater and still greater spiritual power, and it rises now. I am calling many into the great harvest—into my work in my kingdom. Wealth and workers, my children, will rise up as never before since the days in my first century church, and it will be as it was, only much bigger, just as the population of the earth is now much bigger. It is time, like never before, to know my Word, to know my Spirit, to know my Messiah, to know your God.

The days for walking are over. The days for running have come. Dedicate your life to the Lord. Devote yourself to me, your God, and be about my calling, my will, my business, and my Word. Run with me into the work prepared for you since before the foundation of the world. Ask me what I would have you do. Listen to me. Do as I say. Transform your churches so that, though they are many, they will now become one, as it was in the beginning. Run with me, your God, into battle, to the battle line. Lift up the name of your Christ and King. Together we will bind up and heal. Together we will feed, cloth, and house the hungry. Together we will protect and care for the orphans and widows. And with one voice, we will proclaim the good news, that salvation rests in the hands of Jesus Christ, and he gives it freely and generously. Will you join me? Come with me without delay for the time is late and the end nears swiftly. Do not delay; do not doubt. Prepare your hearts for the Lord. Let me fill, complete, and purify your souls, now and forever!

ONE WAY

Friday, May 31, 2013

Many today are saying, find God your way, find him any way—any way you can—any way that is meaningful to you. Call God by any name and worship any way you like. This appeals to those who say inclusiveness and equality are what is most important. Has anyone asked me? Governments and worldly thinking endorse what is called political correctness, but I, God, am not politically correct—never have been, never want to be, never will be. It is I who form governments; governments do not form me. Different faiths, it is said, all worship me—the one true God; but if you do not know me, how can you worship me? If you worship, and pray to, and put your trust in an object made by human hands and your prayers are answered, it is not me answering, but demons. Many evil, lying, and deceiving spirits are sent out into the world by Satan to blur the truth, to water down the foundation of salvation through Christ.

Why did I bother writing my words if anything goes? Why did so many of my disciples die for their faith in me, and still do, if anything goes? Why was Messiah crucified, if anything goes? If all faiths, all religious thinking, all forms of religious practice and worship are directed toward me, then why does Christianity or Judaism even exist? Why did I bother? Why did I lie? That's right, why did I lie? I did not lie! When it is written, "I am the Way," that's exactly what I mean. I did not make a mistake when I said it. When I said mine are the words of life, I spoke the truth. Man's time on the earth has been short and sinful. To redeem men, to cleanse them and purify them, can only be done through Messiah's sacrifice. When I commanded my disciples to go into all the world and preach the gospel, perhaps I needed to qualify that I didn't mean just any gospel. When I said "gospel", I wasn't commanding my disciples to go and preach anything anyone liked, or wanted to believe, or felt comfortable with, or what they had always done, or what was politically correct.

There is nothing more exclusive than being one God and one saving Messiah. I am not ashamed of being exclusive. I am God, I am exclusive, I am one. To be one with me requires you to be in me, and the only way you can be in me is through what the Messiah achieved and won for you by his own blood and suffering! How can I love and teach you to love if I do not love the Messiah? How can I love my adopted sons and daughters if I cannot love my only begotten Son? How can I endorse thinking that says there is nothing special or exclusive about the Messiah—that anything goes—that every religion is equal? When my people were in Egypt, worshipping the gods of their masters, were they worshipping me? Did their gods, made with hands of men, get them out of Egyptian slavery? I am the living God. I am the only God. I am the eternal and almighty God. I AM the only I AM. I made the universe and I AM the only one who can create. You are because I AM. If you declare all religions are the same, you declare all gods are the same. If the Hindu believers want to believe in a god that is a lie, that is their choice; but I will keep telling the truth and I expect my disciples to keep telling the truth. Truth matters. Truth is from me, God. Lies are sourced from the devil and the devil has no life or reward to promise anyone. All the devil can do is lie.

Cling to my Word because it is truth, exclusive truth. I understand that some of you see words expressed that sympathise with those who never get to hear about the Messiah, who never hear the truth, who do not know the way. I understand that I imply that their response to what they see in my creation, whether they praise and honour the creator— whom they do not know, but long to know—will credit them. This is simple justice: that good hearts who, if they had your knowledge, if they heard even a hint about the good news of the Messiah, would run to him. It is justice that such people, who have a strong desire to love me but don't know how exactly, are not deprived because of where and when they were born. However, you are not ignorant. And if you are, you have no reason to be, because you know my Word exists. You can access the truth if you choose to follow me in the way that pleases me. Most people on earth are now like you, in that few are without knowledge of my existence and the existence of my Word.

UNIFY

The promises I made to the children of Israel are trustworthy. My children, the Jews, the children of Abraham, are children of the promise. My promise to Abraham, that all people of the earth will be blessed through his seed, is clearly a spiritual blessing, for what other kind of blessing could it be? And if it is a spiritual blessing, then surely it is the first mention of what the prophets spoke about: that the blessing of salvation will come via the suffering and sacrifice of the Messiah. So it is that the Messiah came first to the Jews and secondly to non-Jews. If the Messiah came to the Jews first, how much do I expect the Jews to accept the sacrifice of the Messiah and be blessed? Children of my friend Abraham, listen, believe, and have faith in the promise, as your father Abraham had, and set your faith in the Messiah.

Like my children, the Jews, I know many good-hearted followers of Islam who love me as their God. You honour me from your heart. Your sincerity shows and I know that you long to be closer and closer to my heart. Do not let the many hateful and insulting things said by your religious teachers and leaders dissuade you. Like all the people of the earth, your ultimate spiritual blessings are found in trusting the Messiah and doing what he says. Read the words of Christ and see if I do not speak through them deeply into your heart. The Messiah and God are one. If you want to be one with me, God, you will find the oneness you seek by becoming one with the Messiah.

My heart overflows with love for all the people of the earth. I am overflowing with love for all of you. I call all worshippers of me, God, to come together to worship me in one spirit, harmonised by love for each other. The Messiah will show you the way if you ask him. The Messiah will give you the power to change, if you will ask him. My children—Jews, Islamists, and Christians—unified and one in the Messiah—will show the world the unity and oneness of God. And many who worship false gods will desire to worship me, the one true and living God, because of your love and unity in the Messiah.

To all devout and sincere Jewish rabbis who know me: arise, stand up, lead the way, show your people the way. You know so much about me that most Christian leaders do not know or understand. You know so much about my Torah and can bring deeper meaning to Christian preachers, teachers, and leaders. You have a long history with me and your knowledge of me, my ways, and my heart will help to unlock deeper knowledge that most Christians do not have about the teachings of Christ.

To all devout and sincere imams who know me: rise and take your rightful leadership role and lead the followers of Islam into unity with Jews and Christians, under the Messiah's reign. Your deep respect for me is of great value for my Christian sons and daughters.

To the pope and leaders of the Roman Catholic Church: I know your love for me, your humble sincerity. Many things trouble you about centuries of decisions made by councils. You know that the church you lead, in its present form, is sincere, but is not the perfect representation of the church that my Son, your Christ, God, died to redeem. The Messiah calls you today to begin the process to reform and transform the Roman Catholic Church into the one church I established—the church that my first century apostles preached, planted, and died for. The Holy Spirit will teach you what must change, what must be done away with, and what must be restored. Humble yourselves before me this day; submit to my authority; ask me to confirm for you that this is my will—my call on your life—to lead, on my behalf, the greatest transformation to the largest and one of the oldest churches of mine, the Roman Catholic Church. I am with you and will bless you; only be about my call for your life and for the church you lead. I will back you with my mighty power; you do not stand alone.

To all worshippers of me on earth: I say that the manner in which you worship—the way it looks or sounds—is unimportant compared to what is in your heart. Worship me in spirit and in truth. The Messiah is truth. The Holy Spirit will guide you into all truth. Set your trust and faith in your salvation through the sacrifice of the Messiah. Do nothing that is not written in my Word and that is not endorsed by the Holy Spirit. There is little written about the shape and form of worship when my children gather together and this is intended to give you freedom to change and adjust to cultures and times, so that meaning and purpose are the priority—the worship, praise, thanksgiving, and glorification of me, God.

To all who read this book, who read these words of mine and cannot understand them or believe them, it has not been given to you to believe—at least not at this time. To all those to whom I grant, from above, the deep knowledge that these are my words and that they are a special blessing to you, be blessed.

May you all desire me passionately as you would a lover. Seek me as a husband seeks a wife, as a wife seeks a husband. Fall deeply and passionately in love with me, as I have with you, and let us be one in heart, one in spirit, both now and for all eternity.

MYSTERIES, SIGNS AND WONDERS

Thursday, June 6, 2013

You call this the age of reason, but intelligence does not qualify you, nor does it necessarily aid you, to please me. In fact, for many, their very perception of being clever is a spiritual stumbling block to them—to knowing my heart personally. For it is the Holy Spirit, and only the Holy Spirit, who brings you as near to my heart as you hunger for and desire. And it is only the Holy Spirit who is authorised to open your eyes, your heart, and your minds to the mystery of God. So it is that some struggle with theologies they consider to be more "clever" than mine—filled with fear, exclusiveness, deceit, ignorance, and confusion.

Some, using their mortal minds only, go to work on our truth as if it were only a question of academics and human intelligence. Yet it has always been through me and, in this age, it will always be through me, that anyone can understand the mysteries written in my Scriptures. So it is that some of my dearly loved children boldly declare that I, God, do not share with people anymore, and that I will not do anything miraculous anymore because I stopped acting with power when the first century apostles, evangelists, and other writers finished writing, and that the last miraculous power from me to heal ceased when the apostles died, and when the last believers who had the apostles' hands laid on them died. Have I become powerless to act? If that is so, why do the missionaries returning from Africa and Asia have to conceal the truth about the power that I pour out and that they so clearly witness?

My children, when I so clearly demonstrate that you have

misinterpreted my Scriptures by performing the very signs and wonders before those who walk among you—the very signs and wonders you say I no longer do—why do you doubt? It is for fear of being shunned, for fear of being cast out of your churches. The churches fear losing their support payments from you, so they feel they must lie. They will not tell the truth that gives me the glory. How much more must I do for you to listen to me. Accept the guidance from the Holy Spirit and praise, honour, and glorify me for what I do on this earth. So it is that you lie, you quench the Holy Spirit, you deny me glory, and you are weak, confused, and condemning of others.

THE GUIDING SPIRIT

Do you not recognise that my Holy Spirit is the unifying Spirit, the reforming Spirit, the Spirit of transformation, the Spirit of oneness? Listen to the Holy Spirit and he will guide you to the heart of your one God—to one truth that founds and holds together, as a unified whole, one church, the one body of my saints who agree because they are all listening to one guide—to one Holy Spirit.

When the Holy Spirit guides you into all truth, you will know that I am the Truth. I want you to know me, for in knowing me, you find your full blessings. When you permit the Holy Spirit to take charge of your life, he assists you with far more than understanding my Scriptures. He shows you your personal sins, weaknesses and failings, and teaches you how to escape these temptations. Each one of my children is unique and I approach you as individuals. What if I want to call you into a particular task that I have for you to do? I call via the Holy Spirit. What if I have a particular person I want you to marry? I tell you via the Holy Spirit. What if you are planning to do something that does not fit my best plans for your life and I do not want you to do it? I send you an uneasy feeling via the Holy Spirit. Or the Holy Spirit simply shares my concerns in your thoughts, if you have the spiritual sensitivity to receive it. What if you are doing something that is right and you want confirmation that you should keep doing it? I inform you via the Holy Spirit through a deep down peace or through clearer methods if you are at the stage where you can receive clearly from me. In your day today, I am keen to guide and steer you, as a father does his children, because I am your Father and you are my children.

Can you not see that the Scriptures are the sound and solid basics—the words of life? But they do not include every application for all the practical living that your life requires. In a similar way, no book can contain all of me. There is so much more for you to know and to love about me. My words are truth; they are like the early stage of getting to know each other, or finding out the basics about each other. The Holy Spirit opens the door of my heart so that you may step in and step up from the basics, to a love and a knowledge of my heart that increases in intimacy as we spend more years sharing our love for each other.

Without the Holy Spirit, you may have a book to argue and fight over, but you lack knowledge, love, all the gifts and fruit of the Spirit, and clearly you lack truth. Wherever there is a lack of truth, there are lies. So it is that my children lie—to support a theology that I prove, over and over, by my power, to be mistaken. I related so clearly that these things will not stop until I am seen face to face—until you know me as you are known by me. Surely it is clear that I will not leave my kingdom without power until it no longer needs my power to battle powerful evil forces that seek to destroy all that is mine. If you feel so clever to work out my truth with your mortal minds, if you feel so clever to be able to guide yourselves into all truth, use your cleverness to ponder this truth: You would not even have my Scriptures to read today if it were not for my mighty power. And were the men at Nicaea not powerfully led by me as they put my available and known words together into what you call the New Testament? Did it happen by itself or out of good hearts alone?

Do you not realise the power of the devil and the battle that rages? If I gave you words without power, then long ago my words and my believers—yes, you too—would have ceased to exist, having been destroyed by the power of the evil one. I love you all and, by the power of Christ's sacrifice, you are my children. But you are as dumb as an ox when it comes to discerning spiritual things and understanding what comes as knowledge from above without the Holy Spirit giving you knowledge, understanding, and guidance in the way of Christ. Listen to him and be wise, my children. Humble yourselves and permit him to guide you into all truth—one truth—so that you may all be one as Father, Son and Spirit are one.

Can you not recognise that there is much which is unclear in my words? Do you not often wonder exactly how things were done and what some of the things and events looked like? Do you wonder if those in the first century knew more than you? You want to and you need to know; but how do you get to know? Ask me, ask your Saviour, Jesus, ask my Holy Spirit. The Holy Spirit is your guide so you are not left guessing and arguing with each other, which leads you into judgement and condemnation of your brothers and sisters. Ask him and he will guide you into all truth.

The Old Testament Torah included a law for the Jewish nation, and don't you wish the New Testament were as comprehensive and as clear? However, as my prophets said, in the last days my Spirit will be poured out on all the people. Are you not in the last days? Although the last days may last two millennia, these are the last days. Seek the counsel of the Holy Spirit; be guided into all truth. However, do not be misguided and deluded into thinking you are hearing from the Holy Spirit when you are listening to your own thoughts. If you cannot hear him, do not pretend; instead, seek out someone who can hear him. Draw close to me. Be humble. Be patient. Ask for my help. I, God, desire to be closer to you than your best friend. To do that, I communicate personally and individually. You can and you will share with me if you desire to come close to me and hunger to know my heart personally. But be certain to not be trapped by your imagination. I will never undermine my truth; I will never lead you away from the safety of my Scriptures. The Holy Spirit will guide you into all truth, to your spiritual benefit—truth that loves, and is patient with your brothers and sisters as we are patient with you—truth that glorifies me, and Christ, and the Holy Spirit—truth that is one, harmonious and unified, as we are one.

What did Peter see when he was sent to the Romans? He saw the

Holy Spirit given. What the Holy Spirit did to the Jews, he did to the Romans. Jewish Christians, after all the teaching of my Son, the Christ, could not lead anyone into my unity by their own knowledge. I led them into unity and I used my Holy Spirit. The very act of me giving the Holy Spirit to the Gentiles was an action of great unity. Without unity, I cannot keep our promise to Abraham. Peter's Christian colleagues argued against him going to the Romans but, when Peter explained what the Holy Spirit did, the brothers agreed and supported the unity of the Holy Spirit. Abraham's promise was safe, not because of Christians, not because of apostles, but because of the Holy Spirit.

Men and women do not bring unity; the Holy Spirit brings unity. Can you not see that man could not redeem himself? I sent Christ to do that. Man could not bring unity himself. I sent the Holy Spirit to do that. If you do not listen to the Holy Spirit, you do not have unity. You do not have unity because you do not listen to Holy Spirit. Peter and his brethren were sincere and loved me, just as you are sincere and love me, but they were not able to walk alone. They were not able to find their own way. They had spent years listening to Christ teach them but that did not make them free agents to stand alone and operate independently of their God. Christ could do nothing apart from me, Father God. You can do nothing apart from the Holy Spirit.

Christ is the Way, the Truth, and the Life, and the Holy Spirit has the light and the sight to show you the way. Follow him. He has the knowledge, wisdom, and truth. Listen to him. No one walks independently on this earth. Either they listen to and follow the devil or they listen to and follow me, God. There are only two destinations: heaven or hell. The way of the devil is easy to find for it is any other way than Christ's. The lies of the devil are anything and everything but the truth of Christ. The death found in the devil is everywhere other than the life found in Christ. The only way to me—the only way to heaven—is through Christ. And the only way to receive all blessings, the abundant life promised by Christ in this life, is by following the Holy Spirit who will faithfully and perfectly lead you into the unity of Christ. I do not expect you to find your own way alone; I know you are not capable of walking alone, finding your own way, and pleasing me. This is why I sent you the Holy Spirit. Listen to him. He will teach you to thrive instead of just survive.

My heart longs and aches for each of you to be in my arms forever. Let's begin today. Can we get together for an hour or two—no distractions—just you and me? Open up the Psalms and let me open up some of my treasures for you to meditate on. Let's chat and share together. Call it prayer, if you like, but let's make it like small talk between close friends. Ask me for what you need but don't forget to ask me for what I think you need—for what I want to give you— because I give generously and I give you more than you can think of asking me for. So cut me loose and give me freedom in your life.

Will you approach me with your intellect and hope to understand me? Will you approach me with your emotions and hope to connect with me? Will you approach me with your best acts and hope to impress me? Please approach me via the guidance of my Holy Spirit whom I have given to you, so that you may find the way of Christ, and so that you may find the only path that leads to eternal life with me. Do not trust your understanding or knowledge, or the understanding and knowledge of anyone else. Only trust what comes from the Holy Spirit and from those who share with you what has been shared with them from the Holy Spirit. It is as it was in the first century. If you want to find me, humble yourself, listen to the Holy Spirit, and set your faith in the salvation purchased for you by the blood and suffering of your Lord, Jesus Christ. If you faithfully listen to the Holy Spirit, he will faithfully lead you into and guarantee you the truth you need, the truth you seek, the truth that sets you free.

What is this thing some of you call slain or slaying in the Spirit? Where did this come from? You may see someone slain in the Spirit and interpret this as a deeply spiritual thing that the Holy Spirit is doing. I will be very gentle here because I know many of you have such good hearts for me. You desire to know me better but you are confused. You want to experience me. You want to be in my arms. I value and appreciate your hearts and your motives if you feel this way, but let me unpack this experience for you and show you what I see and what you are experiencing. Firstly, let me say that I understand people having difficulty standing before me in the flesh. Their first reaction is one of terror from a healthy desire to live and an anticipation of swift death. Even when you are in the Spirit, and not in the flesh, experiencing the divine or angelic beings is overwhelming and terrifying, and I have to strengthen you to endure the experience. Even after we strengthen you, because of your good hearts, you would prefer to bow or fall at our feet, and praise and worship, rather than stand.

So my question to you is this: Are you experiencing a close encounter with me, either in the flesh or in the Spirit? In most cases, the answer is, "No." Your leaders get you excited, your praise music gets you excited, your emotions go out of control, and you follow a pattern that you have seen others do; that is, to fall on your backs onto the floor, usually after a touch or a prayer, and after people have placed themselves behind you to catch you. Doesn't anything about this seem a little contrived to you? It is mostly women because I have made most women more emotionally reactive than men. If it is something that just happens, why doesn't it happen in aisle 3 while you are shopping? Obviously you are not whipped up into an emotional high by others.

Why don't you fall on your face and hurt yourself? Or why don't you fall backwards, anywhere, anytime, regardless of whether someone is conveniently there to catch you? Would I risk injuring you? I am your Father and you are my children. Do you whip your kids into such an emotional high that they are falling down and hyperventilating? Am I the God of disorder? The Holy Spirit guides you into all truth and teaches you to worship in Spirit and in truth. I am sorry, but being slain in the spirit is mostly the product of an overdose of emotions and it achieves nothing spiritual for you. It is rarely something that comes upon you from heaven. Look at your Scriptures and read. The Holy Spirit falling upon masses of believers is rare. And when it does happen, it is for a reason. It is not asked for or expected, and it certainly does not need emotions to be whipped up for it is from me and not from you. The Holy Spirit falling upon masses of believers does happen in modern times, and you know it does. When it is the work of the Holy Spirit, there is no denying it. But the slaying in the spirit that I see in my churches is usually manufactured on a weekly basis, as if the Holy Spirit were there to entertain you and put on a show for you. It certainly is a show; but it is your show and I want you to stop it. I do not need people to pretend spiritual power. I AM spiritual power. Just because I do not use my power as often as you might like me to does not make it right for you to start doing silly things and saying it is me.

If you want to be overcome emotionally by coming near to me in worship and in praise, please do so alone, and one-on-one with me, in the privacy of your own home. Have your passions rise, and glorify, praise, worship and honour me, showing me on the outside how you feel on the inside. But keep it private so that others will not think that you and I are cuckoo. I am not saying you cannot express heartfelt thanks to me in dance and song. Good, happy, and thankful hearts should feel free to express how they feel toward me. My son, King David, did. But all Israel was celebrating a huge victory that I had won for their nation, and they were thankful and could not say thank you quietly. Learn to consult the Holy Spirit on when is the right time, the right way, and the right place.

It is much the same with churches and their healing services and healing ministries. Do I heal today? Of course I do! But clearly I do not heal enough for some of my churches. So they play "let's pretend" and people are getting their sore toe healed. This discredits my power, discredits my church, and discredits me; and I want you to stop doing it. There is nothing worse than a fake to struggling folks who want to believe and want to discover the truth; and instead they keep seeing investigations and reports of false miracles and frauds. People cannot heal. People cannot perform miracles. If there is a genuine miracle from me, it lifts up my name and causes people to believe and have faith in Jesus Christ as their Saviour. Across Africa and Asia, my miraculous power is poured out, often unexpectedly. The dead return to life, the lame walk, the blind see, and demons are driven out. If I want to perform a miracle through your hands, I will tell you, and I will perform that miracle. Until I tell you, stop pretending to perform miracles that are false, shaming my name and weakening faith.

Why have some churches gone crazy about talking in tongues? Some preach that you are not saved unless you speak in tongues. If you use a spiritual tongue, use it at home, privately, one-on-one with me, as it is written. Most want to speak in tongues, so they pretend, encouraged by the hope of being viewed as more spiritual by others. Are there tongues? Yes. Are some using tongues genuinely and correctly? Yes. However, just like falling over and calling it "being slain in the Spirit", making funny noises is also very easy to do, very easy to pretend—and many are pretending. If I have not given you the gift of tongues, stop pretending. You do not bring me glory and you do not bless the church when you pretend, deceive, and lie. Having said this, I know that many of you have very good and sincere hearts. I do not correct you to crush you. I know you were born into this tradition. It was not your doing but you accept it as correct, without exploring Scripture or asking the Holy Spirit, without asking him about what you are doing and what you should be doing. I love you, and you are saved, and you are my children by the blood of Jesus Christ. However, I implore you to come close to the Holy Spirit so that you may be taught more correctly, so that you may come close to me and enjoy spiritual experiences beyond what you can possibly imagine.

RIGHTEOUSNESS

Friday, June 7, 2013

When my Son, Jesus Christ, the Messiah, was anointed for ministry, what did my servant John the Baptiser call out loudly so it could be heard? He cried out, "Behold the Lamb of God who takes away the sins of the world." He did not consider himself worthy to even untie his sandals. Who among you are as holy and righteous as my John the Baptiser? Not a single one of you! John did not feel worthy because he knew no one is worthy. Every mortal pales in comparison to me, God. Every one of you is sinful, broken, fallen. Not one of you is pure, holy, and righteous. Can you save yourself by your own righteousness? Can you stand before me as an equal? Are you one who is holy, righteous, pure, and from heaven? Did you create the world? Did you write the Scriptures?

John knew God in the flesh. The promised Messiah was standing before him. The most junior child servant was given the task of untying the dirty, dusty sandals of his master. Yet John did not feel worthy to be even the most lowly child servant. Most of you, on the other hand, feel so worthy that you don't want to be the one who is the most lowly of servants. In fact, many of you are so arrogant that you tell me about my Word, as if it were your word to do what you want with it. And, in so doing, you do with the Messiah what you want to do with him. You change the Messiah's words of life; you add to and take from the gospel of Christ. You twist and change the words of life spoken to you by me, through the Messiah, the apostles, the evangelists, and others. How dare you come before me with such careless arrogance in your hearts—you who think you can be the authors of a new salvation that appeals more to you and that makes you feel so important.

Do you so easily want to throw away your salvation? Are you better than John? Are you better than Christ? Will you now repent, come before me with a contrite heart, bathe me with your tears, and seek my forgiveness with a thankful heart? Is this the time you have chosen to change your ways? You are my children and how I love you. You stand forgiven of all your sins including these, only because of the Messiah's love, his righteousness, and his generosity to cover your filth with his righteous, pure, and holy garments.

Should the Messiah's generosity to you not melt and humble your heart, and make you want to fall at his feet with your heart filled with thankfulness? Should you not wait for him to pick you up and put you on your feet to stand before him as a forgiven and redeemed child of mine, a child of Father God? Do not despise me, or my Son, or my Holy Spirit with your worldly, arrogant aloofness. Your eternal life is bought and paid for by the blood and suffering of your God. Yours is an adoption by blood, a life for a life—my life for your life. This is how precious you are to me. Show me how precious I am to you. Lift up the Messiah for honour and praise. Seek the Holy Spirit's guidance that you may know what my words say, how to read them correctly, and how to apply them. My words of life come to life in my children, reflecting the life of my Son. But when you pervert my words, only a perverted life walks this earth—not my Son. Others see your confusion and blame me, and accuse Christ. Because you are so bad and ugly at following, while claiming to follow me obediently, others look and conclude that Christ, and the Holy Spirit, and I must be bad and ugly of heart too. Stop giving us a bad name. You produce slander for us instead of praise.

I do not say this to all of you. There are some of you in whom I am well pleased. Listen to the Holy Spirit and he will teach you to live and bring me glory, so that I may be well pleased with you too. Please repent, please transform for my sake—I love you so very much! I have given you everything I have to give. I have spared nothing. Please respond to me in a way that is appropriate and worthy, for your God is great and wants his children to be great too. I will correct you and perfect you, but I will never harm you and will only bless you. The choice is yours. I have chosen to love you. My hope is that you will choose to love me.

ONE BODY

Things can't get any simpler than this: You know that my Son, the Lord Jesus Christ, is the head of his Church. If he is one head, and clearly he is, then he has one body, his church. Which church is his one body? Will you pick one out? Will you tell me that they are all together one church? Surely being divided into many creeds and differing teachings is not one, but many churches. My Son, Christ, may be one head, but you expect him to submit to many bodies—many of which say they are the only, legitimate, one true body.

Why do I say "submit"? Because you are the ones who have made your churches different from the one church you read about in your New Testament. If Christ is to be with you, near you, he must go to where you are, because you are not where he is. He must be married, in oneness, to your diversity, to your lack of oneness. Is there unity in diversity? Oneness is oneness. Diversity is not unity. Diversity is division by another word that you now want to call unity. If you change your terminology and your definition of unity and oneness, you are destroying oneness and unity. Do you create the church or do I? Is it Christ's church or your church? If you died for your church to save all members from their sins, then you are qualified to answer that it is your church. But since you didn't, your answer must be, "It is Christ's church." If you are honest and choose to follow Christ, he will lead you back to the way—his way—where you will find unity in one church. Christ never led you away. My Holy Spirit never led you away. In most cases, you did not exactly lead yourself away either. But you have accepted what has been given to you—a polluted, disjointed church, filled with division—a church so far from its origins that it is significantly different.

I deeply value, respect, and applaud you for worshipping my Son, Christ. You have never forsaken your roots in that fundamental sense. You know who died for your sins. You are clear that faith in Christ's righteousness is your righteousness, and that it is your only way to purity, to approach me, and to be with me forever. Thank goodness my church is not filled with unbelievers. However, I am not represented by disunity. I appreciate your efforts to find unity via a celebration of diversity, because I know you are trying to embrace theological differences, overlook biblical error, and love your brothers and sisters in Christ.

Your love and your efforts are commendable. Nevertheless, why would I leave you in this mess when the church I gave you in the first century was so much more beautiful a bride than the dirty and tattered, shameful bride she is today. I love you too much not to show you the way, not to call you back, not to show you how to get back to what pleases me. I want a beautiful bride for my Son; not a bride full of excuses, full of confusion. There is much to do in my kingdom and the puke of diversity, of disunity, dilutes my light, and diminishes my glory and the glory of my Son enormously.

In my love for you, my dear confused children, I call you back to oneness. My Holy Spirit is here to show you the way. Call upon him; ask him. He is keen to bring you to one teaching, one belief, one faith, one hope, one baptism, one church. If you cannot hear his voice—if you do not know his voice—then find my children who can hear his voice, who know his voice, and who have a heart to follow, to obey, to turn and change, to do exactly as he instructs. This is important. You have been in ignorance for two millennia. But now I am calling you back—clearly, plainly, simply. It is time, my Son comes soon. I urgently and lovingly plead with you to listen and to obey. You have lifted up the different names of your different churches. Now cast off your confusions, your divisions, and be one, as we are one. Assemble under one name, Christ, and lift high his name. Listen to my Holy Spirit who will guide you into one truth so that you may be one body, under the one head, my Son, your Lord Jesus Christ. I have one Son, one church, one kingdom; and one battle rages—join me!

TRANSFORMATION, RESTORATION AND REVOLUTION

Tuesday, July 9, 2013

I lift up many of my much-loved children across the earth—children who I have called into my kingdom to serve—to bring me glory, honour, and praise, and to draw others to me. You hear my voice; you have the thoughts of my Holy Spirit and my Son in your mind. You listen to us, you obey us, and you fellowship with us with a heart like ours. Thank you. You may be wondering why I have not spoken into you the things I now express. My answer is this: You know how my Spirit has so often pointed out Scriptures and made you feel uneasy because you knew that you and your church were not doing them as I wrote them and have taught them. You knew that something was not right because of my Spirit deep within you, confirming that something was wrong and change was needed. But you were never sure what change was needed, and changing a whole church's thinking and tradition seemed impossibly difficult. Now I have made what seemed impossibly difficult into something achievable—if you listen to my Spirit's guidance—if you are willing, and if you do it together in love.

By sending you this letter of correction and by telling you what is wrong and how to make it right by following my Spirit, I have commenced a new season of restoration, of revolution amongst my children in my kingdom so that, together, you will obediently submit to the transformation of the Spirit and go back to the way it was, back to the way of Christ, taught by Jesus the man, and his disciples, apostles, and evangelists.

This letter of mine is to the children of the end of the end times. The time is short, so you must hurry with the Spirit, but the time is right. There is much to be done but, with my power, much can be done very quickly. When I have one unified church, my Son will have command of one army in his kingdom. The whole world will notice the new Spirit in my church—my Spirit. Everyone on the planet will see and know that unity has come to Christianity; the impossible has happened—the church is worshipping and working as one body under one head—Christ. The poor and the downtrodden will praise me for there will be help for them, the impact of which this world has never known.

The fields are ripe but so are the churches. You and every one of my believing children can know how to hear me clearly. I have called many of you for many years through my Spirit, but you have not heard. Ask me for spiritual sensitivity so that you may hear me clearly and know, with confidence, that it is me.

I need you to listen to me and obey. I need you to respond to my calling. Whether to labour for me in my church, or in the surrounding community, or far away in the fields of my kingdom, if I am calling you, I need you to hear me and obey. The first century was amazing. It was not a perfect church because there were some who couldn't or wouldn't listen. But, there were many who did hear me and did obey and, because many did hear me and obeyed my calling on their life, the church of the first century turned their world upside down. It was done by my power, by God power—not man power. I got them excited. They were working as one with me.

Your church traditions are like bad habits. I sympathise because I know bad habits are hard to break. The devil is using your bad habits and your traditions, passed down to you from your fathers, to hold you back from working with me to make the biggest, positive change on this planet that the world has ever seen or known—a change that will have the whole world talking.

Many in the world will envy, be jealous of, despise and resent the church as it rises by my power. Some of my children will struggle with envy and jealousy within my church, as I make choices and call some who others do not approve of. You must control your weaknesses and sinful nature so my Spirit may work within and about you, so that my kingdom may be blessed and not hindered by you.

The world will accuse the church and fear its meteoric rise, but there will be great rejoicing worldwide, as orphans and widows are fed, as children learn to read, as small businesses are established to dignify the poor, as slaves are freed, as the good news of the gospel of Christ is preached to the poor, and as many marvel at the new courage and generosity of my saints the world over. This will be a time never seen since the first century. The bride of Christ, Christ's church, awakens from her slumber, washes her robes, and prepares herself for the arrival of her Groom, the Christ, to join him at the wedding feast. I am preparing you. Today I am calling you to be part of the preparation and purification of my Son's bride—his church. Beginning with you, today, I command the bride to awaken!

Satan is busy in your life. He wants to destroy everything you love. He wants to destroy you and deactivate you, because you have such potential to bring me glory, if you will listen, if you will change. Satan does not want you to listen; he doesn't want you to change. He doesn't want you to stop your secret sin. Satan doesn't want you to love your wife and your children like I love them. Satan doesn't want you to love your husband and your children like I love them. He doesn't want you to love your parents, siblings, neighbours, or friends like I love them. Control your temper; control your mouth. Fill the lives around you with positive, loving, kindness from a servant spirit. Control your immorality, lust, gossip, gluttony; be disciplined and take responsibility.

How can you let me control you if you cannot control yourself? How can you be obedient to me, if you cannot be obedient to yourself? If you have weaknesses, stand in the strength you have in me. Fight back against them and call my mighty power into yourself, so that you may rise in my power, and by my powerful arm, stand obedient and new in Christ. If I am to have my radiant and pure bride, Christ's church, to present to my Son, it begins with you. Open your heart to me. Open up your sin to me. Will I not bring in my forgiveness and my power to change? Alone you cannot do anything to change and bring me glory; but by my power you bring me glory. Yet you must get serious—be determined to follow me, be committed to changing and obeying. Fill your mind with my Word, my Scriptures, every day, so that you may grow to have the mind of Christ.

Empty your life of lusty magazines and internet. Do not watch TV shows or movies that do not endorse my standards. Stop impulse buying and filling your cupboards with more than you need. Don't surround yourself with friends who applaud you, encouraging you to keep your weaknesses, and who encourage you to defy me and not to change. If the fields of your heart are growing a crop of weeds, then bundle them up, take them out of your heart, and burn them. Ask me for my seed and I will plant in the field of your heart a crop that, when harvested, will bless you and everyone around you, everywhere and forever. I say honour your preachers and elders; honour your authorities and others in roles that serve you—teachers, nurses, police officers, soldiers, garbage men. I say to you, change. Stand in the strength you have. Show your heart—do your part.

Beware of the fast-approaching deceptions of the devil who, using signs and wonders, will deceive many, resulting in many worshipping him and mistaking him for my Son, Christ. See, I have spoken; I have warned you this day. Turn to my Word, the Scriptures, your Old and New Testaments. Read them; become familiar with them. Understand that your Christ will return, as it is written. No one else will arrive like my Christ. If anyone tries to tell you that they are the Christ, or that the Christ has arrived, and invites you to come and see, do not believe them because it is a lie. Christ will return just as it is written and you will need no one to tell you he has come. Many will be fooled by the devil and his servants because they do not know what my Scriptures say, or because they do not believe that my Scriptures are my Word. I have warned you in advance so that you will not be fooled and cheated out of your reward.

The devil is more actively preparing his plans and now is the time when my church should listen as one person to my Holy Spirit, so that it may function under one head, my Son, the Lord Jesus Christ. You are an indispensable part of church oneness because every part of the body must be connected and joined to the head, Christ, for the church to respond as one being, as one bride. Join me, listen to my Spirit, and be one with me.

David, son of man, my champion, you have proved faithful in writing my words; yet this is but the beginning of you helping them, in my name, to be one with me. As I have been with you, David, so I will be with them. Go in the strength you have, stand and walk in my power, run to the battle line, helping them to hear me, giving them confidence as they hear the voice of my Spirit, and nurturing their courage as they reform their churches to breathe as one with me, and my Son, and my Spirit. Arise and go, for I go with you. Hurry now— run with me, as you help guide them to be one with me, your God and their God. Teach them in love. I love you and I treasure you. I love you all, always!

CHANGE AND REFORMATION

Wednesday, July 10, 2013

Do not despair! I have given you all you need. You have my Spirit within you. You have your salvation in my Son. You have all you need. I have been harsh on you—not to make you give up, but to jolt you, to catch your attention, to get you to listen to me. Today I give you permission to change. Some of your organisations are big, and have been around for centuries, and were established by great men. So who are you to change them? To remain unchanged is a mistake—a mistake that feels too comfortable and acceptable to be a mistake. To change, to reform, to transform, creates fear. If you leave my church as it is, you don't have to stand for anything. You don't have to take a risk. You can just keep on doing what everyone is doing—the same old, same old.

But this is not just about change. This is about my command to you to change. I am commanding you that my will is for you to change, and to remain in my will, you will change. I am not asking you to do something new, but to do as it was—to do what my Son commanded you, to do what my apostles taught you, which is what I had taught them. This is not about change for the sake of change, or changing because you are bored, or because there is a better way to appeal or to get more numbers in. This is change that has no risk for you. The risk for you is to remain the same and refuse to change. If anyone takes any risk here, it is me. I am the one commanding you. I am the one telling you to listen to the guidance of the Holy Spirit so that you may have the confidence that you are pleasing me, that you are in my will, that you are following my teachings and obeying my commands. My transformation, my reformation of my church, is all about my love for you. If you do what I am instructing, you will have a relationship with me, and with your brothers and sisters in Christ, that is closer and more fulfilling than you ever thought possible.

Trust me, when you have left the best way, there is only one direction that is good, and that is to turn around and move back to the best way of Christ. And there is only one who can be your guide back, and that is the Holy Spirit. It is the Holy Spirit's responsibility—not yours. All you have to do is have a good obedient heart; ask, listen, and act. My Word is already written and is true. All you have to do is implement it in your own life and in the church. Jesus already is the Way. You have the Holy Spirit to show you the way and to keep you in the way. All that is left for you to do is desire. Your desire—your heart for me—will be shown in your obedience to me. Hear me today and do what I say, because I love you, always!

You may think that you have all you need right now and you are content with the way it is for you spiritually and relationally with me, with my Son, and with the Holy Spirit. But you do not know what you are missing. My Son's words are life, because they come from me, and I am life. When you have partly my words and partly the opinions of men, you are part alive and part dead. You may feel comfortable with that because you have never known anything better. But this is written at this time to cause you to lift up your eyes to me, because I have so much more for you than you have today. I want you to have the very best. I want you to enjoy the whole feast, to be fully spiritually nourished, and not left half filled, half weak, half strong.

This is not just about you, even though it begins with you, but it is about the whole world. Half the world, half filled, half weak, half strong, is not what my Son died for. We love the whole world. We want to seek and to save all the lost. If we can fill you—not half fill you, but fill you so that you are overflowing with us, overflowing with us into the church—then the church will overflow with us into the world, the whole world. What will result is the greatest spiritual revival the world has ever seen or known, and lives will be blessed without measure.

You may worship with a church where you feel very alive spiritually, where you are ministered to by men and women who you feel are very alive spiritually. Until you have spiritual intimacy with me, you lack the relationship it takes to completely please me and to completely please yourself. You will be left dissatisfied. You will try to fill your dissatisfaction through trying to get closer to me in worship at your church, but intimacy with me, and my Son, and my Spirit are not found in exciting spiritual experiences at church. This is why you go home and you return to the same feeling that something is missing. You do not feel complete, you do not feel completely filled, you lack deep down, spiritual satisfaction.

I want you to have what you lack. I want you to have all of me. I want to have all of you. I want spiritual intimacy with you. You have to be deliberate to achieve the closeness of a spiritual relationship that is intimate with me. If you want to experience the rush, tingles and goosebumps that even your physical body feels when your spirit and my Spirit touch, you have to be deliberate. Firstly, you must empty yourself of the world in every way you can and fill up on me in every way you can. TV and Facebook are replaced with reading my Scriptures, watching online sermons, listening to praise, or listening to my Word read aloud, rather than listening to your radio or your popular music on disc. I need to get into your world and into your head, before I can get into your heart. You want more of me, but I want more of you, and I need more from you. You have got to be deliberate.

My heart wants at least 30 to 60 minutes one-on-one with you every day, but does your heart desire to give me that? My Spirit will urge you to give me more quality time. Every time your eyes see or your ears hear things that water down or joke about morals and spiritual things that are qualities I admire, you are undermining me and my Son in your life, and you are subjecting your heart to things that hurt my heart and your heart. If you want brilliant light from me in your life, you have to stop letting the world in to dim it. If you want, in your mind and in your heart, my words and the words of my Son, which are the words of life, then you have to stop watching, reading, and listening to words, opinions, and images that replace our words of life with stuff that has no life or value in them.

If you are not deliberate, you are like a person who wants to be close to someone—who wants a close friendship, who gets to know what is in their heart and mind, what makes them tick, what they like or don't like—but you also feel completely comfortable choosing the company of others who mock and laugh at your best friend behind their back. Would you like to find out your wife or your husband was doing that to you? You would feel hurt and wonder where their heart was. My Son and I feel the same. Be deliberate. Don't say you want closeness with us, but then live and manage your life in a way that only distances you from us, and only makes you a closer friend to the world.

We cannot achieve everything we want to achieve by changing the church, without first changing our relationship with everyone in the church, you included. My Holy Spirit wants to guide you, but you have to walk with him in the way of Christ; and to do that, you cannot leave one foot standing in the world. You cannot choose closeness with me and also choose closeness with the world. That is impossible because the world hates me. You have to be deliberate. You have to choose. I hope you choose me, and my Son, and my Holy Spirit. We are here to help you, as are my faithful children who are filled with my Spirit.

Section Two

HOW TO
GET CLOSER
TO GOD

WHO IS CLOSE TO GOD?

Firstly, who do you know who is close to God? The name of your preacher, pastor or priest may come to your mind. But are you assuming they are close to God because they are a leader in a church, or are they truly close to God? It's reasonable to expect that people who have their degree from a Bible or Ministry College are close to God. People who know their Bible well and pray a lot must know God well, right? Sadly, the reality is that most church leaders find themselves so busy and short on time that they get little time to slow down and just chill with God. Most of their engagement religiously is spent doing what they are obligated to do, such as sermon preparation, visiting the sick, learning, planning and implementing new ways of growing their church, growing the faith of members, growing youth numbers, and increasing the giving. When they are not doing these things, they are devoting time to their marriage and spending time with their children. Often there is little time left for God after meeting the needs and expectations of their church and their family.

In the busyness of ministry life, time rushes by and relationships with God, wife/husband, and children can easily drift unintentionally into a crisis. The demands of most busy people in ministry ironically crowd out God and spiritual connection to God. Then, when tests, trials, and challenges present themselves, because they are in a weakened spiritual state, they will all too easily become part of the sinful mess, rather than be filled with the wisdom and guidance of the Holy Spirit. Like the people in ministry, we can be busy doing many good things—many good works—but if we neglect our relationship with our God, we are not doing a good thing and it will end badly.

God's methods do not always ensure a short term victory. But if we are in God's will and under his instruction, we avoid sin, God is pleased, and that matters more than short term victories. Churches break, split, and splinter when spiritually broken people try to do the job of spiritually healed people. The Lord's work is done the Lord's way when we are close to God, have the mind of Christ, and listen to and implement the personal, trustworthy guidance of the Holy Spirit.

Most of us are busy—too busy. Lack of time weakens everyone's marriage and relationships. It is not just a lack of time but, more importantly, a lack of quality time, intimate time. This means time spent one-on-one with nothing to do but enjoying spending time together: time for small-talk, for love, for noticing and appreciating what you love about the other person. This is essential in marriage, in our parental relationships with our kids, and in our relationship with God.

Reading the Bible is good and necessary, as is praying and worshipping at home and at church. But does that deliver what you and God are really wanting and needing? Intimacy is not a book, or a prayer, or praise, or worship. It may incorporate all these things, but these are not intimacy. If you want intimacy with God and have tried to find it, you know that it is more than these good things because, after you have done heaps of all these things, you are still left wanting more. And it is not these good things that you want more of; you are left wanting more intimacy.

So what is intimacy with God and how do we get it? Intimacy with anyone, including God, is spiritual in nature. It is felt deep within, as either a longing or a hunger for someone if we are not getting enough intimacy, or as a deeply satisfying sense of thankfulness, appreciation, and completeness when we are getting enough intimacy. Clearly, by the design of God, we are created with the capacity and the need to function at some level of intimacy. All we need is the desire to do so. All of us desire the deep satisfaction that is derived from achieving intimacy with something or someone. Whatever we pursue with the greatest passion is likely to be what we are either intimately hungering for (if we are not getting enough of it), or deeply and intimately content with (if we are getting enough of it and feeling filled).

If we have competing intimacies, we have to trade for more of one and settle for less of another. Our greatest hunger or satisfaction may focus on our qualifications, our fame, our house and things, our money and investments, our wife/husband, our children and grandchildren, and/or our God. The questions are: What do we desire and hunger for? And can we get enough of it to feel filled, content, and deeply satisfied?

If qualifications, money, career and self are our greatest loves, then our marriage, family, and God relationships will be left to starve for intimacy. Our hearts are not big enough, and we do not have enough time or energy to achieve intimacy with everything and everyone we like; so we have to choose.

If we make the wrong choice, thinking that money and things will deeply satisfy, and later find out that we cannot get enough to satisfy our hunger for more, then, fortunately, we can choose again. If we turn to people and God for intimate relationships, we will need to learn how to not just want to receive it, but also how to give it. Intimacy with others is not a one way street. Intimacy is shared—both giving—both receiving—both having their hunger satisfied. There are equal numbers of selfish women and selfish men who want to receive without giving. Good relationships and intimacy are the product of work and effort, whether they are with other people or with God. We reap what we sow. If we do not put much in, we should not expect much out. Relationships and intimacy are not a free lunch.

The very best that comes from the heart of another, comes freely; it should not be forced or shamed out of people. Men and women need to be reminded of what God has designed them to be. Yet, we do not benefit from constant reminders of how inadequate we are. God does not constantly put us down. God knows what we are capable of. Men and women are created to love. Our love is broken and faulty because we are broken and faulty. But we can do better and, as we try harder, we see the positive results that God knows will come. If we open our minds frequently to God's Word and our hearts frequently to God's love, we and others will be blessed. If you cannot love sufficiently, ask God for his powerful, loving help. If we ask God, he will pour his love into our marriage and into our family. When men and women are humble before God and humble before each other, good things happen!

I hear it said that God will always satisfy, but this isn't necessarily true. In fact, I think God frequently disappoints and does not satisfy, because we are expecting the wrong things, or we expect to receive everything good that we ask for. Someone we love may be dying. We want them to be healed and to live. We pray, knowing that we are asking for a good thing, but God doesn't give it, and we doubt his love. We wonder if he cares; we wonder if he was even listening or interested. This is a question of the will of God. We usually do not know much about what is in God's mind. We see a small picture if he chooses to show us. We must permit God to work freely, according to his will, because he knows it all; he sees the whole picture. We must not limit God to our knowledge and to our will, or the outcome would not be good for any of us. Life hurts. That's because of the devil, not God. God brings his love into our hearts and fills us with peace and hope. He soothes our hurts.

People who seek money and things for their satisfaction must continually seek more and more, because it always takes more to satisfy them. But isn't it the same when we seek God? When we start out, it doesn't take much of God in our lives to satisfy us. But to keep us satisfied, we seek more and more of God in our lives. Jesus himself said, "Blessed are those who hunger and thirst after righteousness, for they will be filled." So Jesus used the analogy of hunger for the physical food that our bodies need to help us understand our hunger and need for righteousness and spiritual satisfaction. Food is needed every day for our physical health, and spiritual food is required every day for our spiritual health. Not only this, but food helps us grow. As we grow, we change and this requires a change in the type of food and the amount of food we eat. So it is that, if we want spiritual growth, we must stay hungry for more of God and keep pressing in for more intimacy.

We can share space and time with our wife/husband and with God, and not grow in intimacy, because intimacy is not just doing time or hanging around together; it is intentional. When we are intimate, we are "not-to-be-disturbed"—it is private time. It is about love. It is one-on-one time. It is focussed. When we are with God, it is as if we come together in one spirit—to be one. In a marriage, the couple will come together in harmony, to be unified, to be best friends, determined to make their future together better and happier for each other.

In relationships between dads/mums and their children and grandchildren, there is a need for closeness. There is an intimacy in our relationship with our kids, but naturally not sexual intimacy. Our kids are made in our image, as it were. They are formed out of us—bone of our bones—flesh of our flesh. How we feel as dads and mums is similar to the way God feels about us. We need a deep connection, at a heart level, to feel complete and satisfied.

The need for intimacy and capacity for intimacy is clearly part of our design. What about God? He does not have a design because he does not have a designer. However, he does have a make-up, a personality, and character traits. The way we are made hint at who God is because we are made in his image.

In sexual intimacy with our wife/husband, we can experience a sense of oneness that can transcend the physical. No longer are we sure of where we or our wife/husband begin or end physically because our experience has become more spiritual than physical. It is in the spiritual experience where we find oneness. How did we begin the intimate encounter? Maybe spontaneously; but most likely it was planned, arranged, and it didn't happen by chance.

Before enjoying intimacy with your wife/husband, you probably choose the time and setting in advance so you will not be disturbed. You prepare with a shower, brush your teeth, and change your clothes to look nice and smell nice. You may prepare some tasty snacks and drinks. You play romantic music, dim the lights, and simply enjoy chilling out together on a comfy couch for half an hour or an hour—nibbling on the snacks, sipping on your drinks, sharing small talk, cuddling up together, being affectionate, touching each other's hair and face. Little by little, as it feels right, you respond to each other. Everything—every step of the way—is enjoyed, and you end up deeply satisfied, blessed, and your hunger for intimacy is finally complete—until next time.

Intimacy with God is much the same. Sometimes it may just happen spontaneously as if by chance, but usually it is intentional. Making time at a do-not-disturb location is part of the basics because you will certainly want to be left alone with God. There is no specified time to be set: it may be 30 or 60 minutes or it may be two or three hours in duration. It continues until you and God are satisfied and your hunger for intimacy with each other is finally complete—until next time. You may wish to listen to some beautiful songs of praise; you may want some snacks and something to sip on; you might read some Scripture. You may enjoy some small talk, taking the form of praise and complementing God, Jesus, and the Holy Spirit on how gentle they are, how kind and sweet they are, and how much you long to be closer and closer to them because you want to be one with them. You may dull the lights, relax, and simply savour and meditate on the goodness of God.

After a while, you may find that God takes the lead and asks you to pray—without words. You will be still and silent and allow God to assist you to sense him spiritually. In this spiritual state, slowly strengthening as it is moved by your God, you will experience a oneness with God that is so deeply satisfying that you feel filled, at peace, and without hunger—until next time. When you don't know where you end and God begins, nor where God ends and you begin, you are in a spiritual state that you do not want to come out of. Every time you are out of that state, your heart aches for your God to be up close and personal. You long to see him, and to be with him as he really is—in his glory—and to be, forever and ever, inseparably with him. In human terms, intimacy between us and God is best described as a romantic, spiritual experience.

Some men may wonder if it is harder for a man to experience this than a woman because God sounds male. Yet, such thoughts are not true because God is spirit. You are not engaging a man or a male. For over three thousand years, great men and courageous warriors have experienced God in this way, and have come away from tasting the heart of God, saying that he is sweet.

Some have used the term "mystic" to describe those who walk and talk with God and experience him personally, but a close friendship with God does not need labels. Some say God only talks to certain people and not to everyone. But I suggest that it is more God who initiates closeness with us, and that it is usually us who frustrate intimacy between us and God. God is a keen lover and we are the ones who play catch up, but he is delighted to lead the way and teach us how. If we but glance in his direction, he will come running. If we will give him but a small part of the time and attention we give to a person we are falling in love with, God will reward our efforts generously, leaving us filled, content, and satisfied. If we desire to fall madly, head-over-heels in love with our God, he does not play hard to get, but nurtures our love, encouraging us to grow in our intimate love for him.

We can hear and believe, repent and be baptised, lead a moral life based on Scripture, worship, give to the needs of the poor and, with faith in the righteousness of Jesus Christ to cover our sins, God is faithful to keep his promises and give us eternity in heaven with him. That may be enough for some of us. But you are probably like me in that, when you see the relationship that Jesus had with God while he was walking this earth, and the relationship the apostles had with Jesus, the Holy Spirit, and God, then you want what they had. If I cannot have that because God doesn't do that anymore, or because God doesn't want to do that with me, I will accept that. However, if I can have more and more closeness with God's heart, I want that! And most of you are just like me because we can never get enough of the sweetness of God. The more you get to taste his heart, the more you want to taste his heart again and again and again! Thankfully, God wants our hearts to be so close to his, that he tastes his sweetness in us. What a mighty, loving, and gentle heart our God has for us. Oh, that his love will fill our hearts and that the overflow of his love in us will taste sweet to our God.

Using the term "mystic" to describe a person who enjoys close friendship with God makes it sound mystical, but it isn't. It is natural and normal love with our God who is love! It takes time to grow. It cannot be rushed. If you are not experiencing what I am describing, then probably all you need to do is give away your television set, and give God one hour a day for spiritual pleasure with you. Time devoted to watching television is one of the key reasons why so many people today lack spiritual intimacy with God. Perhaps most evenings you are still at work making money, or you are at the gym, or training, or playing a sport, or out with friends or with your wife/husband/kids. Whatever it is, you can probably give God 30 to 60 minutes each day of distraction-free, one-on-one time, if you plan to—if you earnestly desire to.

If you cannot, then I suggest you take the time and make the effort necessary to rearrange your life so that you can, because the deepest pleasure and satisfaction is found in God himself. If you can fit two to four hours in with God every day, without neglecting your relationships with the nearest and dearest human loves of your life, then do it. You can talk with God about anything and everything because you have the very best lover, the very best friend, and the very best teacher there is. Enjoy him to the fullest.

Having suggested the above, I should add that, leading up to, and since my calling and anointing to put down God's words in this book, a heightened spiritual experience has occurred, where clarity of communication has increased significantly. You and many other people on this earth may experience God far more than I do, and many may experience God differently than the ways he has chosen for me. This is not about you or me. Our desire for intimacy with God is clearly very important, but ultimately, it is all about the desire of God and the will of God. My experience is that God is willing—very willing! Just as every close, human relationship shows both similarities and special uniqueness, it appears, from what we read in Scripture and what we experience in life, that our close relationships with God also show both similarities and special uniqueness. You and I are sure to experience both similar and different things as we draw closer and closer to God and his sweet heart.

Each of us is like a new, living tabernacle—a temple of the Holy Spirit—a human Holy of Holies, where God's Holy Spirit resides (1 Corinthians 3:16; 6:19). Christ will come in and eat with us, which is clearly describing fellowship and friendship, so we can expect sharing and communication (Revelation 3:20). John 14:23 describes God and Christ making their home with us. The social intentions of the Father and the Son are to be up close and personal. Nevertheless, they may not place their thoughts in our heads, nor may we hear any words. Perhaps their communication will take the form of an inner peace, or a lack of peace if we are doing the wrong thing or about to do the wrong thing. God most commonly shares with us as we read Scripture, often guiding our thoughts through the Holy Spirit and expanding our understanding in ways that are not obvious to us. Whatever way God chooses to share with us, we can be sure that he will and, at the very least, desires and attempts to share with us. We know that good dads always love time with their children, and love sharing, chatting, teaching, and laughing with their kids. If we are in Christ, we are God's children, and God, being the very best Dad, will surely share with us. He will always be very near and will never leave us.

We know that communication between people takes different forms. A scowl or a pointed finger can communicate heaps, as do smiles and laughter. A wink and lots of other body language mean something significant within a culture or family; they usually know instantly what it means. Sometimes God chooses to use very different ways to communicate exactly what he needs to convey to us. Sometimes God shares because we need to know something from him. Sometimes it will be something he needs us to do for him. Other times it is something he wants to do for us.

I recall one of those times when God communicated differently to me. It occurred on Monday, March 11, at 12:30 p.m. I will do my best to describe something that is difficult to find the right words for. I was in my kitchen alone, enjoying a moment of worship. I reached for the fridge door to get some milk to make a coffee, and had to stop, then and there, to lift my heart to God in praise and worship. As my heart lifted to his and as my good thoughts of appreciation and praise lifted to him, I felt the arms, the lips, and the breath of my God. His arms were warm, his kiss was gentle, and his breath was warm and natural. I had a feeling of euphoric ecstasy. It was like being in the womb of God—his blood flowing through me—his breath was my breath—we were inseparably one—where I ended and where he began I could not tell. I said to my God, "Thank you; you are everything thrilling, good, and beautiful. You are the most wonderful and exciting thing that ever happen to me. My best moments, best feelings, and best times are in your arms, with you—in you. I feel you inside me and I feel me inside you. It feels perfect, complete. Your thoughts feel like my thoughts. I don't feel me or have an awareness of me, but I feel you and only have awareness of you. Like an empty vessel, I feel filled and overflowing in you and I feel washed away by you. I don't care what other people think. I have found love. I have found my lover. I have found perfect and complete love in the One who loves me perfectly and completely. There is nothing better, nothing higher, nothing greater. I have it all. I want nothing else. Thank you, my beautiful God, lover of my soul, lover of me. Thank you."

I know of no one who communicates love like God. My wife and I enjoy love and intimacy, and it feels good; it feels similar to a passionate embrace with God, but God has other dimensions and power and ability. An embrace from God feels like it touches every part of you all at once—body, mind, emotions and spirit. But God communicates his love in lots of ways. He gives us happy marriages, happy children, good friends, good food, clothing and shelter, jobs and careers. He gives us everything we are and everything we have. He shows his love for us in infinite ways.

FOSTERING INTIMACY WITH GOD

Some characteristics of intimacy with God are visible in public places too. The New Testament records the now famous "Martha, Martha" incident, involving Jesus, Mary and Martha. Luke was not present, but there is no evidence that those who were there ever disputed his account, given in Luke 10:38-42. [New International Version]

> *"As Jesus and his disciples were on their way, he came to a village where a woman named Martha opened her home to him. She had a sister called Mary, who sat at the Lord's feet listening to what he said. But Martha was distracted by all the preparations that had to be made. She came to him and asked, 'Lord, don't you care that my sister has left me to do the work by myself? Tell her to help me!'*
>
> *"'Martha, Martha,' the Lord answered, 'you are worried and upset about many things, but few things are needed—or indeed only one, Mary has chosen what is better, and it will not be taken away from her.'"*

Martha was very busy doing all the work, preparing the food and drinks for Jesus and his disciples, and it is reasonable to assume that Martha was working hard to ensure her guests feel honoured by her generous and thoughtful hospitality. There is no reason to doubt that Martha was doing a very good job with all the preparations.

Meanwhile, Mary was not in the kitchen helping her sister but, instead, verse 39 states that she "sat at the Lord's feet listening to what he said." Mary was free of any possible distractions and appeared to be captivated by what Jesus was saying.

Most of us reading this will know what it is like to be in love, and will recall listening like we had never listened before as the person we loved spoke, and as we tried to remember and treasure every word. We normally have a keen interest in a person we love and their words are very important to us, because we are learning all about them and want to know how to please them. I am not suggesting that there is anything physical about the love that is prompting Mary's behaviour, but she is exhibiting all the signs that there is something powerfully spiritual that is motivating her desire to be positioned where she is, listening to Jesus. Of course, in Jesus' case, his words are not intended to encourage her toward an earthly marriage to him but, nonetheless, his words are intentionally and unavoidably the most unique that Mary will have ever heard.

Jesus' words were special because they were words from heaven—words his Father God had spoken to him. Jesus told his disciples, in John 8:28, "I do nothing on my own but speak just what the Father has taught." And again in John 14:10 Jesus said, "The words I say to you I do not speak on my own authority. Rather, it is the Father, living in me, who is doing his work."

One of the signs of Jesus' intimacy with his Father while he was on earth was Father God talking to him. Similarly, one of the signs of Jesus' intimacy with Mary (and the disciples) that day, was Jesus simply talking to her. When we read God's Word, we begin to fall in love with our God and his Word, and when we hear him speak into us, we fall even deeper in love, and are drawn closer and closer into spiritual intimacy with him. For us, as human beings, chatting and sharing our thoughts are important to falling in love. Likewise, chatting and sharing our thoughts with God are important to falling in love with God the Father and the Lord Jesus Christ. We first fall in love with their words found in Scripture; then we fall in love with their hearts—the source of their words. Finally, we fall in love with the divine essence of who they are, which is pure love.

Again, this is so similar to human relationships, where intimate love is found, because we first fall in love with the words of the man or the woman who God brings into our life, before we fall in love with their heart. I expect it is safe to conclude that Mary was madly in love with Jesus—not in a sexual way—but she was entranced and captivated by her growing trust in knowing that she was at the feet of divinity and receiving words from his mouth and his heart. Her head was in his classroom but her heart was beginning to beat as one with his. So it is with us: God's Word is such a wonderful vehicle for whetting our heart with an insatiable appetite for the heart of our God. It is a love for his heart that takes our breath away, for his love—his heart—is like no other; it overflows with love that never fails, never disappoints, never stops, but is ours eternally.

Undoubtedly, Mary was enjoying a wonderful spiritual time with Jesus, but what about Martha? The house was full of guests, and it can be assumed that normally Mary and Martha would have combined their efforts and shared the work between them. But not this time! Mary was captivated with Jesus' teaching, to the exclusion of helping Martha. And just like all of us, if we were in her situation, Martha didn't like it. If it were a young man/young woman type situation, the only way they could have mixed their infatuation with responsibilities, would be if the visiting young man or young woman noticed the growing frustration and suggested that, together, they help in the kitchen. Jesus could have suggested that he and Mary help Martha in the kitchen, but he didn't. It wouldn't have been hard to help and teach or listen, because the kitchen was probably in the same room. Jesus, Mary, and Martha could have prepared and served the food together, and Jesus could have kept on talking to his disciples, teaching them precious spiritual insights coming to him from Father God.

However, there are two valuable things that Mary would have missed if she had helped Martha, and Jesus wanted her to have them, because both are essential to intimacy and more important than keeping customary good manners and social responsibilities. The first valuable thing she would have lost by helping Martha was her physical closeness to Jesus. She was in a prime position and, out of all the places that may have been available for her to sit, she chose to sit as close as possible to Jesus. She was not trying to get out of work, and she was not trying to pose; she was simply driven by a sincere desire in her heart to be close to Jesus. The second valuable thing she would have lost by helping Martha was her undivided attention. Had she moved away to help Martha, Mary would have had to divide her attention between what Jesus was teaching and the food preparations. From her close position at Jesus' feet, there was nothing between her and Jesus—nothing going on that would be competing for her mind, her thoughts, her attention. Mary chose intimacy and Jesus did not refuse to give it to her. When Jesus said, "Martha, Martha, you are worried and upset about many things, but few things are needed—or indeed only one. Mary has chosen what is better, and it will not be taken away from her," it is probable that Jesus' desire for Martha was that she leave the kitchen duties, sit with Mary at his feet, and that after the teaching, everyone would quickly prepare the food and drinks together, ensuring that everyone gained the maximum value from the occasion, and no one was left out. However, Jesus did not suggest this to Martha. It seems that those who hunger for intimacy with God will not be denied it; but for those who do not, God will wait until they do.

As human beings, we have natural physical needs. Among other things, we must eat and drink to sustain our physical bodies. If we are hungry, we will actively search for food. We want to satisfy our hunger. If we are thirsty for water, we seek it, because we want to quench our thirst.

Similarly, when we are empty and aching for intimacy with God, we seek him out, because we have a need that will not go away until it is satisfied, and the only thing that satisfies it, is intimacy with God. When God created the earth, he made it with water and food to supply our physical needs. We may see our work and our pay as the means for buying our food at the shops, but God has provided our earnings.

Also, if he hadn't created food and water, there would be no food to buy at the shops; there would be no life on earth.

Intimacy with God is clearly a spiritual need, for God satisfies it generously, as he does our physical needs. We bring to God our desire, our need, our hunger for intimacy with him, and he generously satisfies it. In God's spiritual intimacy, we are not left to starve and wither, but to grow strong and thrive.

Christ's ministry was regularly punctuated with praise and thanksgiving to Father God. The writings of the apostle Paul were also punctuated with praise and thanksgiving to Christ.

If we are in love with someone, we think of all the positives. Our thoughts dwell on how great they are and how happy they make us feel because they are so lovely. We think of the many things we like about them, and how perfectly happy we feel when we are with them. And, like Jesus and Paul, when we love God, we must do the same. We must think of all the positives, how great he is, how happy he makes us feel, how lovely he is, and how perfectly happy we feel when we are with him.

We need to fill our head, the whole day through, with how good God, Christ, and the Holy Spirit are, how much their presence thrills us, how they never leave us, how they never leave us feeling empty or alone, and how they whet our appetite for being with them one-on-one, encouraging our longing for intimacy with them. Like with Mary, what you desire, you will receive, if your desire is for something good. Intimacy with God is something very good.

Most of us have tried to diet, and we know that dieting and thinking about food do not mix. If we fill our head with thoughts of food, we are going to break our diet, because our mind and our thoughts are powerful. The last thing we want is a God-diet! We need to fill our thoughts with our loving and kind God, so that we stay hungry and thirsty, and keep our desire for God whet with anticipation for our next intimate time one-on-one with him

In Matthew 6:31-32, Jesus said, "So do not worry, saying, 'What shall we eat?' or 'What shall we drink?' or 'What shall we wear?'… your heavenly Father knows that you need [these things]." Jesus assures us that we can trust God to supply our physical needs; how much more so can we trust God to supply our spiritual needs? God knows we need spiritual intimacy with him and he provides it. He will not leave us spiritually starving, aching, and empty. God desires intimacy with us more than we do with him, and he will come running into our arms.

Sadly, most of those whom Jesus healed during his ministry did not follow him and did not seek to join his inner circle. There is no indication that any ever tried to repay him with a donation, or accommodation, or meals, or transportation. Jesus healed them, gave them a whole new life—a new beginning—but how many came back and insisted on getting close to him, wanted to hang out with him, or wanted to know him better? How many came back with a heart overflowing in gratitude and love for the one who had healed them? Are we like that too? We are spiritually healed. We are given a whole new life. Do we just walk away with the gifts—with the blessings—and call over our shoulder, "Thanks Jesus!" and keep on walking? Or do we want to hang around, stay close, and never be apart from him? Does the very fact that we are saved from our sins and are heaven bound cause us to fall madly and passionately in love with the only one in the universe who feels like that about us—the only one who has ever, or will ever do that for us—and the only one who will ever suffer a horrific death to spare us so that we may live? Do we just walk away from our baptism dripping, shrugging it off, and keep walking farther? Or do we run back into his arms because no one loves us the way he does, and no one ever will? It is our choice. Intimacy is our choice.

Because you are reading this, God wants you to have everything he has in his heart for you. Salvation is a wonderful gift and a heart that gives such a costly gift is a heart you never want to walk away from. It is a heart that has so much in it for you, and salvation is only the beginning of your everlasting intimate love story with God.

In the West, we have much; we abound in stuff and things. However, our poverty in God is very evident. We see in Scripture the apostle Paul talking about the spiritually rich being physically poor. Most likely, if we prosper physically, we are poor spiritually. In 2 Corinthians 8:1-9, we read:

> *"And now, brothers and sisters, we want you to know about the grace that God has given the Macedonian churches. In the midst of a very severe trial, their overflowing joy and their extreme poverty welled up in rich generosity. For I testify that they gave as much as they were able, and even beyond their ability. Entirely on their own, they urgently pleaded with us for the privilege of sharing in this service to the Lord's people. And they exceeded our expectations: They gave themselves first of all to the Lord, and then by the will of God also to us. So we urged Titus, just as he had earlier made a beginning, to bring also to completion this act of grace on your part. But since you excel in everything—in faith, in speech, in knowledge, in complete earnestness and in the love we have kindled in you—see that you also excel in this grace of giving.*
>
> *"I am not commanding you, but I want to test the sincerity of your love by comparing it with the earnestness of others. For you know the grace of our Lord Jesus Christ, that though he was rich, yet for your sake he became poor, so that you through his poverty might become rich."*

The poorest Christians, the poorest churches, can also be the most generous. In the West, we are inclined to cling to our stuff, our things, and our money. The more we have, the more we have to cling to. God wants us to cling to him and we cannot, at the same time, cling to money, stuff, and things. God is a jealous lover. He dislikes it when we focus on our money instead of on him. When we have a divided heart—when our love is for another or for something other than God— he walks us along a journey in life that helps us lessen our love for other things, while increasing our love for only him, Christ and the Holy Spirit. He wants faithful lovers, faithful hearts, not hearts that have others waiting in the wings in case our relationship with him fails or hits a rough patch. If we run out of faith in God, will we fall back to our faith in our money, our investments, and our financial independence? If we do, we are running back to our other lover—to our first love: our money, our stuff and our things. Jesus knows our heart, and he calls us to love him, Father God, and the Holy Spirit above everyone and everything else. In Luke 14:26-27 Jesus says, "If anyone comes to me and does not hate father and mother, wife and children, brothers and sisters—yes, even their own life—such a person cannot be my disciple. And whoever does not carry their cross and follow me cannot be my disciple." It is our choice.

Do not despair if, right at this moment, you honestly know that you do not love God above all else. God loves hearts that are keen to grow and Christ sympathises with our weaknesses. If we have a great desire to know God intimately, we will get to know the love of God. When we fall in love with God and understand his irresistible love for us, we will draw closer and closer to him. When we are close to God, we find everything we need to please him. We also obtain everything we need from him, including his forgiveness for all the areas in which we have missed the mark and fallen short of his expectations. God understands that the only one who can love him as he deserves, and who can please him completely, is the Lord Jesus Christ, who is God in the form of a man. Only he could do what is impossible for us. A great price has been paid for our sins and it was not paid so that we may easily be condemned to hell. We should take heart, for God loves us and he understands our frailties. He forgives us when we hurt him and disappoint him. Therefore, we must also forgive others when they hurt us and disappoint us. When we love others, we love God. Our love for others is a very important expression of, and evidence of, our love for God.

Let's look for a moment at Christ's intimacy with Father God. He shows that the less of the world we have, the more of God we get. Jesus' ministry began with his baptism. We read in Matthew 4:1-4:

> *"Then Jesus was led by the Spirit into the wilderness to be tempted by the devil. After fasting forty days and forty nights, he was hungry. The tempter came to him and said, 'If you are the Son of God, tell these stones to become bread.'*
>
> *"Jesus answered, 'It is written: Man shall not live on bread alone, but on every word that comes from the mouth of God.'"*

Christ's encounter with Satan continued until Satan left and angels attended him (verse 11). My point is that, as Jesus became weaker physically, he became stronger spiritually. He was one-on-one with Father God. He was experiencing deep spiritual intimacy with Father God. Essentially, Satan's temptations were designed to break Christ's intimacy with and dependence on God. Satan was jealous of the intimacy.

We see the same thing from Satan in the Garden of Eden, where he was successful in breaking Adam and Eve's intimacy with and dependence on God. Worship of God involves intimacy with and dependence upon him. Christ died to restore our intimacy with and dependence on God. It is no wonder that we are encouraged to participate fully in this rich and eternal gift that is ours right now, here on earth, and that continues on into heavenly eternity.

Just as Satan tried to separate Adam and Eve, and Jesus from intimacy with God, he can be expected to subtly try to take us out of God's arms too. But Christ offers us his righteousness, the purest oneness, the most precious love, a relationship, an intimacy that is like an intricately-woven fabric that cannot easily be broken; it is made strong by its many strands. Our intimacy with God and Christ is our most important relationship. But God, in his love, knows our need for relationships and does not call us to separate from our wife, our husband, our children, our grandchildren, or our friends. Instead, in Luke 10:27, Christ says, "'Love the Lord your God with all your heart and with all your soul and with all your strength and with all your mind'; and, 'Love your neighbour as yourself.'" Jesus is telling us about the importance of loving God, ourselves, and others. God loves marriages, families, and friendships that overflow with his love. God's love and intimacy does not bring division, but rather a shared unity and oneness into all our nearest and dearest relationships.

God is supreme because of his supreme love. In his mighty love, he sent his Son to redeem us. Because of his mighty love, his Son said "yes" to redeeming us, bearing our shame, our pain, and our brokenness so that we may be healed, healthy, and full of joyful confidence in the arms of our God, in the passionate embrace of our Christ. God's love does not come without passion. God is passionate; his love is determined. He searches us out, he finds us, he re-creates us, he raises us up through Christ's holy blood, making us pure lovers, worthy and fit to be in God's arms, to hear him breathe and to feel his heart beat. We can snuggle close beside him and know that we are safe and at peace. This kind of safety and peace cannot be found anywhere else, or in the arms of anyone else. He is the only one who can provide it.

Right now we can have a taste of heaven on earth when we are in the arms of our God—in the arms of our Christ—bathed in their love. One of the most beautiful things I know is when my God whispers into me, "I love you." He says it so tenderly, so gently, so kindly; he says it like he means it—as if I mean the world to him. It sends chills through me and gives me goose bumps. I feel the blood rush to my stomach, saliva floods my mouth, I feel a bit dizzy, and I just want to fall into his arms and be completely one with him forever and ever, and ever.

His own heart, his own life, his own love is available right now, to each of us personally, here on earth. It is our little foretaste of heaven—our heaven teaser, our sampler, the passing aroma, the tiny taste whetting our appetites, making us want to plunge eternally into God's love for us. What he has for us now is such a powerful "WOW" that we cannot even imagine what awaits us later, as we walk into heaven, never to depart again, to be with our lover of all lovers, eternally.

I am putting this in terms of God the Father, but this is not to the exclusion of Christ and the Holy Spirit, for they are also God. They are one, and our complete joy is found in their oneness with each other and with us. In the power of God's love is our power to thrive and to drive his kingdom forward in his way, always asking and listening to him. As it was with Jesus, every word we say, must first come from the lips of our Father God, and everything we do, must first be seen being done by our Father God. In this way, Jesus was assured of pleasing his Father. In the same way, we are assured of pleasing our Father God. We show our heart for him when we want to please him. His love for us empowers us and strengthens us to live and grow, and to bring him glory in all we do, as we harmonise in unity and oneness with him. Until we are one with our God and find spiritual intimacy with him, we cannot find oneness with our brothers and sisters; that is, with all the worldwide family of believers in God.

Our oneness with God is contagious, just as it was in the first century. Jesus' oneness with Father God affected the lives of the apostles, and they brought that oneness with God to all who heard them and believed. Church, worship, giving, and evangelism all fall short and fall flat without oneness with God. If we do not have oneness with God, we are only able to share words like clinical academics; we only have theory and head knowledge without the experiences and personal knowledge of the living God. When our words are God's words, they are God's truth and they have power. And when we have intimacy and oneness with God and Christ, we talk about what we know, who we know, and what we experience, and we become sincerely influential, as Jesus and the apostles were. When we are one with God, with him personally, we harmonise with his organisation and his plans; we function as one living God organism. The bride of Christ—the church—is meant to be living in oneness, in intimacy, and in revival, with a worldwide bursting forth of the latter day rains, for the huge harvest of all harvests that was prophesied so long ago.

We now live in the end of the end times. This is the time when we will see and experience the living power of God on this earth through his church. The living power of almighty God is at work in each of us, radiating from God and Christ, through us, into the whole world, via the Holy Spirit. God's plans are more than exciting and far bigger than we can possibly imagine. They include the final and complete fulfilment of all that the prophets spoke of, all that Christ and the apostles spoke of, and all that the first century church was excited about—the very return of Christ for us, the children of the most high God. The time is near for us to be caught up into the clouds with Christ and to bring us—his church, his bride—in through the gates of heaven. We will see our Father God in his awesome glory, as we approach the throne of grace with confidence, to be invited into the most amazing and powerfully loving embrace we have ever experienced and will ever experience. It will be the eternal embrace, as lovers with God, in true and complete oneness. This is for you; this is for me; this is the gift given to us and bought with the blood of Jesus, so that we may be one with him, Father God, and the Holy Spirit, in intimacy, forever and ever, and ever. God's indulgent generosity is beyond measure. It is too much. God is too much. In heaven, as we look at who sits before us—our God, in his glory, on his throne—we will feel unworthy, perhaps even deeply embarrassed to be so undeserving, yet offered so much. We may be thinking that this is what we have longed for our whole life and know that he is really before us and our eyes are truly beholding him. We may hesitate, and we may need to look at the face of Christ for encouragement and permission to step forward confidently. Yet, we will approach, for he is irresistible—completely and totally irresistible.

The one we cannot resist on earth is the same one we cannot resist in heaven. Maybe we would feel more comfortable being kept at a distance. If it were formal and we were kept back, and only permitted to be present at a distance, and to fall to our knees and worship him, then we might feel that our presence is more appropriate. But God is not that kind of God! He longs for the hearts of his children, his lovers, and he longs to have us in his arms. We cannot stay back. We cannot stay back now and we will not be able to stay back later. Our God is the personal God, the intimate God, who wants it all. He wants all of us, individually and collectively, and there is no running away—no hiding at a distance. We are to enjoy the personal and individual experience of being in his arms, now and always. This is what you and I were created for. This is what Satan stole from you and me. This is what Jesus died to buy back for us. God is not the far away daddy, but the close and personal daddy. We are to resemble our Father and give to others as he gives to us, as he teaches us, and as he shows us his love and how to love others.

It begins at home. As you read this, you can adapt it to your life. God personally tells me to love my wife, to show her I love her, to tell her I love her, to touch her gently and affectionately, and to cuddle her frequently. I do this to my wife more than she does to me, but this is what God has created me to do and to be; so I am simply being me. My wife of over 39 years loves being loved by a man who is trying to love a little like God—a man who fails, but who tries. My wife tells me I love more than anyone she knows. God has taught me more than I have learned from anyone else how to love my wife. He made us. We did not make ourselves and we do not know what we need. We all have ideas of what we need and want, but only God knows what will truly and deeply satisfy us. If we listen, we will learn. God will teach us his love and show us how to love ourselves and each other. We are faulty and will fail, but if we keep trying and failing, and trying and failing, we will eventually do better.

The best is, most certainly, still to come. But what is here right now for us is astoundingly and breathtakingly exquisite. We should not fear. We should not live in disbelief. We should not hesitate. The heart of our Father God, the heart of our Lord Jesus Christ, and the heart of our Holy Spirit await our love with open arms. Like little children, we do not need to know very much at all about what we are doing; we only need to let sincere love and the Word of God be our faithful guide to the heart of God, and he will take it from there. Why would we hold anything back? All God is asking from us is our undivided affection, our undivided attention, and our love. As broken, fickle and faulty as we may be, our God longs and aches for our love.

We have already given him all our rebukes, all our rejection, all our rebellion. We are just as guilty for Christ's death as the Jews and Romans were, nearly 2,000 years ago, for we have all sinned and are saved by his sacrifice. We took the 30 pieces of silver and led the soldiers to where he was, and we kissed the cheek of our friend Jesus to identify him. As we walked away alone into the darkness, he was marched away alone with his enemies. We have held the whip and lashed his back with all our strength, all our might. No light or merciful strokes came from us, only heavy ones that stripped the flesh from his back until his bones were bare. We placed a royal robe on him and mocked him. We wove the thorns into a crown, forced it down onto his head, looked into his eyes and watched the blood drip. We punched his face until he was almost unrecognisable. We hammered the nails through his hands and his feet. We made him suffer and squirm in pain. And after he died, we held the spear, aimed it, and thrust it deep into his side to make sure we had killed him. We have broken the heart of our Father God, and we have shattered the body and broken the heart of our Lord Jesus Christ.

Many times we have sobbed over our sin, cried because of our carelessness to our God, and every time we are extended their forgiveness and kindness. Today, our sins and failures remind our Saviour of his great suffering. We open up his wounds when we sin, and cause him renewed sorrow and suffering. But he forgives us every time we fail him, picks us up and encourages us to not grovel in our shame, but to rise up in his victorious righteousness.

In order to be intimate, we must recognise our guilt and shame. To own what we have done is vitally important. We will never know the forgiveness granted to us if we do not know our guilt. We will never know our freedom if we do not recognise our captivity to sin. We will never know the weight of our sins, until we see the ugliness of who we are and what we have done, contrasted with the beauty and loveliness of Christ. We know what we deserve. We cannot value only what we have been spared from, which is hell, but we must understand what we have been given, which is nothing less than the very heart of God, and an intimate relationship with him now and forever. Although we have given them such sorrow and pain, our Father God and our Lord Jesus Christ give to us their love and welcome us into their hearts. They are vulnerable to us hurting them over and over again because we are weak and we sin. Yet they would rather be vulnerable and hurt by us, than cast us away. They will heal us, strengthen us, and raise us up to be the children we should be—the children we truly are—children of the most high God, adopted brothers and sisters of our Lord Jesus Christ.

This is not an opportunity to squander. Their love is not something to take lightly. To be loved so very much by the only perfect ones—Father God, Jesus Christ, and the Holy Spirit—to be family with the makers of heaven, the makers of our eternal home, to be trusted as friends of the divine ones, to be trusted with their hearts, their happiness, their satisfaction—is an honour that is hard to believe is ours after all we have failed to be to them. This is a marriage. We are in a divine marriage. We bring our sins that hurt them, and they bring their divine love that fills us to overflowing with everything we have ever longed for but could never find in ourselves. Their love is not found in stuff, and things, and money.

The Father, the Son, and the Holy Spirit are everything we have ached for, but our aching is over. They are the ones we hunger and thirst for to fill us to overflowing, but we hunger and thirst no more. It is not fair that we should receive the gift of their generosity after all we have done, but this is the result of the intimacy of all intimacies. It does not exist because of us and it will not be denied us because of who we are. It is because of God himself and his mighty heart, overflowing in perfect and pure love for us. It is simply decreed. He has spoken it and therefore it is. As the universe was made by the words of God, so our intimacy, and all the gifts that go with it eternally, are decreed by God. God chooses to love his enemies and to offer salvation and forgiveness to those who hate him. God is love and he cannot do anything else than love us. Otherwise he would not be God. So we are the beneficiaries. Our God and our Lord Jesus Christ, bring to us their love and their hearts, and spread them before us like a love feast, so that we can wine and dine on their flesh and their blood, as it were. In this way, we spiritually drink and feast on their divine love, and taste their divine hearts, allowing us to know that they are sweet and impossible to resist.

What will we do with God? He comes to us with arms wide open, with hands outstretched and full of gifts from above, and with a heart brimming over with love for us. But what should we do? Just love him! There is nothing else we can do, except love him. He pours into our hearts, into our minds, and into our lives, his love—so much pure love that there is love to spare. With his exceedingly abundant, pure love, we love him back, and we love others like they have never been loved before. We love Father God like Jesus showed us while he walked this earth as a man. He taught us how to love God, ourselves and others, like God loves, even while we are in our mortal bodies. Like Jesus, we turn the world upside down with his love, beginning with our nearest and dearest, then our brothers and sisters, then our neighbours, and not forgetting our enemies. And, like Jesus, we listen and do what we are told by our divine sources above: to love, to listen, and to do as we hear from heaven. The mind and heart of our God in heaven is to be released through us—through his church—to all people. What a thrilling privilege this is! He gives us his love to love with. He gives us his words to hear and to do what he says. By his love, and with his instructions and his power, we will see the latter rains begin to fall. We will witness the worldwide revival, we will participate in the revolution to end all revolutions, and we will see the church become one, unified under Christ. Together as one, we will rise to meet him in the sky when he comes for us. What a blessed generation we are: the generation that does not grow old, the generation that will see the dead in Christ rise first, the generation that will leave this earth to enter heaven. There is much to be done before we leave, so that none will be left behind. We know that there will be many who choose not to listen, just as there were in the first century. As there were those who refused to listen to Jesus and the apostles then, there will be those who refuse to listen now. But for those who believe, let us prepare our hearts for intimacy, and our churches for headship under Christ, so that we may all be found ready for the return of our Lord Jesus.

Section Three

WHY ARE WE PRAYING FOR BUT NOT SEEING REVIVAL?

US FIRST!

Revival starts with us. We all have to get revived before we can expect to see a worldwide revival.

Revival will not come from just working harder, from doing more of the same, from doing church better, or from spending more money. We want what happened in the first century—that's what we really want. What we saw in the first century was lots of enthusiasm and the power of the Holy Spirit. Enthusiasm alone is not enough. The Holy Spirit guides us into all truth and, as we drink in his Scriptures and act upon them, we obtain the mind of Christ. Without this, we cannot sow an unadulterated seed. It is only the seed of Christ—the words of life— that have the power and impact. But we have to be impacted first; we must have his seed growing in us. Otherwise we are all talk and no action—we are like the world—we are like everybody else and not like Christ.

The Holy Spirit takes his word into our hearts and goes to work, changing us into the people God and Christ need for their work to be accomplished. The Holy Spirit will not take the teachings of men into our heart and give them his power. So if we have partly the teachings of men and partly the teachings of God, then we only have part of the power of the Holy Spirit. We don't want or need part—we want it all. The Holy Spirit only works powerfully when it is his words and his will. Then we get his power.

Most churches should have at least a few brothers and sisters who hear from God clearly, and who can advise on church reformation and revision, in order to help transform his church back to the way it was intended when it was fully under Christ and the Holy Spirit. Not that it isn't under Christ and Holy Spirit now; it is just convoluted, so to speak, because we are rather rubbery when it comes to being under Christ and the Holy Spirit. We are the church, but we do not do all God says, so we rob ourselves and his church. If some of Christ's teachings and some of the apostles' teachings didn't matter, they wouldn't be there. We cannot play God by deciding that some teachings are important and other teachings are not. We don't know what we are losing, what we are missing out on, because we are not God.

In the first century, the teachings were there, intimacy with the Holy Spirit was there, and the church exploded because the power of God is explosive. If our hearts are fully for God, we will listen to the Holy Spirit, and the rest is God's department. We have all played with the Scriptures without the Holy Spirit, and the best that has resulted is a silly game of academics where no one agrees with anyone else. So, playing academics kills unity and passion, and this just isn't the way it was intended to be.

If we take part truth, or even a whole lot of truth and a whole lot of love, we can get a whole lot of growth. But what if we let the Holy Spirit guide us into all truth? What if the power of the Holy Spirit was allowed to be poured into the churches—into the kingdom—the likes of which have not been seen since the first century? We would see the worldwide revival that we have been praying for, because the Holy Spirit is ready and willing.

Maybe our prayers for worldwide revival are not being answered because we are waiting for God to do something, when God is waiting for us to come close, to listen, and to do!

So it is that we pray for worldwide revival and keep praying for revival, but don't get worldwide revival. Instead, we get the same-old-same-old. For over 50 years, Christians have asked God for worldwide revival. One hundred years before that, God was also asked for worldwide revival. Is God slow? Are we the only ones that want worldwide revival? Doesn't God care about worldwide revival?

Maybe God's silence is his answer. Maybe he is waiting for his church to wake up—to revive! What is the point in God adding to the church as it is today? We want the return of the first century times; we want it the way it was when Jesus was here. We want a first century God, and Christ, and the Holy Spirit, but we are not ready for that because we are not a first century church. We are not running and functioning according to God's church pattern, God's church design. If we purchase a washing machine, microwave, phone, camera, laptop, car, or watch, we get a user manual with it. We read that to learn how to operate it. If it isn't working properly because we are not operating it according to its maker's design, then we have to adjust how we are operating it. We have to go back to the manual, read it, cooperate with its design, and harmonise our behaviour with the mind of the designer to get it to function the way it was designed to.

The same goes for God's church. God, with Christ, is the designer—the maker. He made it to achieve a result that is deeply satisfying to Christians on earth, that is God and Christ glorifying, and that presents the body of Christ—his children, the church—as a beautiful radiant bride, ready for the return of the Bridegroom, Christ.

So how do we run the church according to God's and Christ's design? The simple answer is, we don't. We were never intended to. The church is in a mess and no longer resembles the maker's design because we, the people of the church, have been trying to run it for nearly 2,000 years. The moment we began trying to run it, was the moment we began to lose sight of the church maker's manual, and the church no longer thrived to the glory of God or Christ. Yes, we are saved by faith in Christ; but most churches and Christians are sadly spiritual survivors, rather than spiritual thrivers.

So why would God add an enormous number of new saints to our churches? Why would he add to our mess and make our mess even bigger and less functional, and, at the same time, give us the impression that we are pleasing him and getting our revival prayers answered?

If we desire worldwide revival, we must first revive the church by reforming it back to the original pattern. Churches that do reform and transform, will begin to thrive; and churches that do not transform, will continue to only survive. In this way, God will show that his way is the best way and the only way. We are in the very last of the last days. It is time for churches to transform to the original design.

Some churches are loving, enthusiastic, very gracious, and grow bigger and faster than other churches because the love of Christ is very attractive. But what if our "big and thriving", were little more than God's "small and confused"? Do we know what it is to spiritually thrive? Are we comparing the sprinting pace of spiritual cripples and we don't even know it? Have we tried sincerely to make the church better but, in the process, unwittingly gotten in God's way, slowed him down, and hindered him? Are our prayers for revival somewhat like us inviting God to join our church, while he waits patiently for us to join his church? Is there a spiritual Mexican standoff occurring, but we just can't see it?

If we have done, or not done, things already made known to us by God in his Scriptures, then we are disobedient—we are sinning—we are missing out on blessings, and we need to correct what we are doing wrong. Of key concern is the overt role that the Holy Spirit played in the management of churches in the first century. We manage our churches very differently today. If we were to propose first century church management, most church leaders today would consider us crazy. Unfortunately, what is considered crazy today was, in the first century, called faith in Christ, trust in God, and dependence on the leadership and power of the Holy Spirit. So it was that the appointment of church elders, preachers, teachers, evangelists, and deacons was by the Holy Spirit, via the drawing of straws, etc., or via men who were being directed by the Holy Spirit. Similarly, in the Old Testament, God chose King Saul and King David via the prophet Samuel. The Holy Spirit preferred to appoint men, rather than women, to positions of authority and leadership in the church. Today we can expect the Holy Spirit to show a similar first century preference for men in leadership. However, the important thing is not the gender of the person chosen, but the fact that the person chosen is the choice of the Holy Spirit.

Some argue that today we go by the New Testament and not by the Holy Spirit. But recent research reveals that the first century churches had more New Testament gospels and letters circulating than most of us realise. It was not long before the New Testament began to take form, so there is not a large difference between us today and believers in the first century as far as Scriptures go. The biggest difference between us today and believers in the first century, when it comes to appointments and management of the church, is their dependence on the Holy Spirit compared to our independent and self-confident thinking that we can place the right people in the right positions better than God can.

Our confidence extends into knowledge of Scripture. We feel that we know enough, and that God has already given us every blessing by giving us his Word. So we think we have all we need and can continue on our way, independent and separate from God, as long as we do what God's Word says. Understandably, without God at our side, we have messed up.

The New Testament is nothing like Mosaic Law. From what God tells me, it is no mistake or accident that the New Testament is a muddle. God could have easily given us something clearly laid out and organised; but instead, we have a mishmash of information that can be quite elusive and resistant to pinning down. In fact, the New Testament seems to be full of traps, and we have fallen into most of them. We overemphasise one thing at the expense of another. Or we build a whole theology around one principle or commandment and, in the process, pull everything else out of shape. Scripture is spiritual and is written by the spiritual mind of our God. We need a spiritual mind to unravel and release the blessings. We need the mind of Christ. And part of being like Christ is not being in independence from God, but in dependence on God, for even when Jesus spoke, he spoke the words of God the Father, so we know his mind was inseparable from the mind of God in all things, including Scripture knowledge, decision making, and living in general. We should imitate Christ.

The very manner in which the New Testament is written testifies to the fact that God expects us to rely on the Holy Spirit in all spiritual matters, rather than live in spiritual independence. We need the Holy Spirit to help us draw from Scripture every valuable blessing that God has for us. The very manner of the presentation and structure of the New Testament keeps us dependent on God for our spiritual knowledge, our spiritual blessings, and our spiritual relationship. We need God.

As it is, all of us, to some degree, have abandoned the church maker's instructions, and not a single church operates and functions according to the pattern intended by God. We all believe different things. We all practise different things. None of us fully follow Christ or live by the New Testament under the guidance and balance of the Holy Spirit. None of us know how to fully integrate the Old Testament and the New Testament in the manner intended by God. With earthly and unspiritual minds, we have twisted, distorted, and bent Scripture out of shape into a pattern that appears good to us. We have added to Scripture and taken from Scripture. And because we all pick and choose differently from Scripture, the church today is cursed with struggles and squabbles. Today the church is not one, and we know it.

God be praised, for there are some church leaders and some churches that are waking up to this big weakness in our churches today. They are trying to get closer to God, to Christ, and they are seeking the Holy Spirit's direction in all matters. We all need to follow the Holy Spirit's compass back to where the church can be blessed and thrive. Churches that are already seeking transformation guided by the

Holy Spirit are beginning to thrive. There is no holding back the Holy Spirit. He will keep urging, he will keep encouraging, but he will not force. The Holy Spirit should not have to force us to listen and act to transform.

When Jesus left, he clearly showed the importance of the Holy Spirit's powerful role. Jesus was only one man when he walked this earth in a man's body. He was only in one place at one time. This was a leadership limitation that did not fit a "go into all the world" international kingdom. Jesus was departing from the earth, but he said that the believers would be better off because the Holy Spirit would be sent. The Holy Spirit would be our guide, helper, comforter—our strength and power from God—to enable us to stay in God's will, to stay within God's purpose, to hold us together as one. We did go into all the world, but it was not long before we were preaching slightly different gospels, beginning to operate slightly different churches, and generally doing things our own way, rather than staying close to God and doing things his way and by his power.

We were given this mess of churches. We didn't do it; it happened long ago. And this is not about being saved or not being saved. This is an opportunity given to us from God himself—a call to transform—a voice calling to us to get back to the Way, Christ's way. We have got to stop trying to find the way by our own efforts. Our church fathers, by their own efforts, got us into this mess. The Holy Spirit is the only one authorised by God to lead the way out. He is the only one who knows what is right and what is not. The Holy Spirit will never lead us to breach what is written in the New Testament because he wrote it. We have trusted in ourselves. We have trusted in men and, because of this, the church is not the church of the first century. We have presented many excuses but none take away our inner guilt, because the Holy Spirit testifies to our spirit that we must change together and worship God as one people with one voice. Then, and only then, will Christ be glorified in his kingdom, as God intended.

Satan does not want you to read this book and he is furious that, through this book, God is calling for all churches to come back under the Holy Spirit's powerful guidance. Just as the power of God has battled against the devil and won, to see this book go out, so the enemy of God will try to tear out of your heart the powerful truth that God is trying to sow and grow in your heart. Let us not hinder Christ from receiving, at his return, his powerful and radiant bride—the church he died for in order to save it and set it free. God loves us as his children. We are bought with the blood of Christ. It is now time to sit, with the Holy Spirit at our side, to restore the design of the church to the maker's pattern, so that he will recognise his "Christ-made" mark on his church when he returns.

It is your God-given choice, but I pray that, under consultation with the Holy Spirit, you will hear the call of God going out to you, to me, and to all believers worldwide, encouraging reform back to the first century church pattern, so that God and Christ may be glorified.

MAINTAIN FOCUS AND
HAVE GOD CONFIDENCE

We do our best work for God when our minds are focussed on him—on his stated will for us—and on his promises and faithfulness. However, how often do we let our attention be distracted away from him? We need to be on guard, for even that which is good and worthy can take us captive like the things of the world. Nothing is worthy of taking our eyes off Jesus or our focus off our God. We must be aware of distractions from our personal love story with our God. Religious and theological matters can also distract, and we must keep our focus on Jesus Christ and on Father God. Churches can easily get distracted by the "best church" debate, or Theological Fundamentalism vs. Liberalism debate, or the did Jesus drink alcohol debate, or the smoking of cigarettes debate, or the makeup and jewellery and hair length debate, or the tattoo debate, or the cleavage and skirt length debate, or the gluttony, obesity, and gossip debate. Focussing on God, being guided by the Holy Spirit into what Christ wants for his church and for us individually, and walking with the Holy Spirit into an understanding of how to apply the truths of the Bible in love, are basic essentials if we seek to please God in order to receive the best God has for us.

Remember, Satan is smart and deliberate. It is not by accident that our minds are often filled with every reason why we are garbage, why we cannot be confident, why it is impossible for us to be happy, why it's not possible to be nice and only possible to be nasty. The fruit of the Spirit—love, joy, peace, forbearance, kindness, goodness, faithfulness, gentleness and self-control—are all things that Satan hates and he is doing everything to stomp these out of your life.

If you are listening to everything negative, everything that's determined to kill your passion, that's stealing your enthusiasm, and that's destroying your confidence, then most likely you are hearing from the devil. Or you are listening to your memories, sculpted by your past, in which the devil has been stomping you down for a long time. Listen to God. Don't listen to the devil. The devil is not just about trying to tempt you to do the wrong thing; but he is also very keen to stop you from acting and rising up to do the right thing—to do God's thing. The devil is loud in our ears. But God's thoughts, the Holy Spirit's guidance, come subtly and we require spiritual sensitivity to hear them, which is a gift from God. Do not be shut down by the devil but draw close to God. Let Christ inside you because he wants to work inside you and explode out of you.

God is confident and assured; not arrogant, boastful, and conceited. God's confidence is a perfect mix with a kind and caring attitude. When you are filled with God, when Christ explodes out of you, you will go with a presence that exudes a kind, joyful, positive confidence. God knows his children are powerful in his kingdom when they are listening to him and when they are like him. The devil knows that too, and he will try to reduce you to someone who is too scared to squeak at their own shadow. The devil will even try to convince you that acting withdrawn and shy is a sign of humility. It's not. Our pride should be in our mighty God. This comes when we are hearing and following the Holy Spirit, when we know the Scriptures, when we keep them and live them out. When we keep company with almighty God, his confidence in us and in his plans for us rub off.

The world has an ugly confidence and boasts arrogantly in its sinfulness and its pride, but God's confidence helped turn the world upside down. The apostles and all the disciples were told to wait in Jerusalem for the Holy Spirit to be given. The power of the Holy Spirit entered into those good-hearted, sincere men and changed them from frightened deniers of Christ into mighty leaders of the early church.

The change in these men was powerfully impressive, and even the Jewish leaders noticed and commented. When you know God's purpose for your life, when you know he is for you, when you know you are pleasing him and that you are close to him and following his lead, you are confident in all things that are from God. From the first moment on the field, you look like you have already won and you exude success, because you are on God's winning team and you share the victory that Christ has already won for us.

The devil cannot shut down God. When God rises inside you, you rise. When God activates you, you take action. Choose the one you will listen to: God or the devil. Know God's Word, know God's voice. Learn to wait patiently. Ask for and use God's power to change your life, so that you may have the mind of Christ and do the works your Father planned for you to do before the world was created. You can be confident that Satan will do all he is permitted to do to try to hold you back from a life that glorifies God and blesses others. But God is more powerful than the devil; so the power that is for you is far greater than the power that is against you. Make God the owner of your mind and your thoughts. Read your Bible to learn the way God thinks; then think that way and only that way. Ask for and receive guidance from the Holy Spirit and obey him.

Never be fooled. God will never contradict his Scriptures, so you must read them and know them. Practise using God's power to overcome your weaknesses and sinful nature, beginning with the people you live with and the people you see every day. Show people the nature of God by the way you think, the way you speak, the way you act, and the way you love. When you have learned to use God's power to live like God on the inside and on the outside, you can be sure that, at the right time, God will use you to represent him in bigger and bigger ways, and you will be used to bless others as God's nature flows through and out of you into the lives of everyone around you. May God bless you in this. You are so precious that the one who made the whole universe died so you can live!

Becoming one and feeling as one is going to be tough. We may think we have the mind of Christ; but if we did, we would all be so different, and so would the church, and the whole world. The fact is that, for thousands of years, we have been looking over our shoulder in suspicion of other brothers and sisters, or looking down our noses at our brothers and sisters, and at the world, and thinking we are better. We have been living according to a delusion which amounts to thinking that our sin doesn't stink like that of others; in fact, our own filth has a hint of perfume to it. Many generations of this mindset have made this thinking acceptable to us, and we have forgotten that it is evil thinking according to God.

LOVE AND FORGIVE

This warped and judgemental thinking places our souls in danger. When we think, feel, and act this way, aren't we being the unforgiving servant as described by Jesus himself. Jesus was warning Peter, who was one of his close friends; so we can be sure it applies to us too. Out of love for us, Jesus gave us an intentionally graphic and horrific warning when he said to Peter,

> *"Then the master called the servant in. 'You wicked servant,' he said, 'I cancelled all that debt of yours because you begged me to. Shouldn't you have had mercy on your fellow servant just as I had on you?' In anger his master handed him over to the jailers to be tortured, until he should pay back all he owed.*
>
> *"This is how my Heavenly Father will treat each of you unless you forgive your brother or sister from your heart." (Matthew 18:32-35)*

I think it is wise and honest to think of our sin debt to God as being hopelessly impossible for us to ever pay off. Mine is probably infinite trillions in dollar terms, while yours is probably much less than mine, but still equally impossible to ever pay back. We can never pay heaven's entry fee; so why, in our right minds, would we ever want to risk being stuck with that bill? You and I do not want to stand before God, with heaven in view, and be found morally bankrupt. We do not want to pay off the debt of our own sins in hell. We want Christ to pay them off for us so we can enjoy heaven. We place our own eternity in the balance when we will not walk in loving harmony with our brothers and sisters. We must kindly encourage everyone to know and live out God's Word, as we walk in intimacy with God, and listen to and accept the guidance of the Holy Spirit. Peter had to listen to the wise counsel of Jesus that was coming from Father God. Today we listen to the wise counsel of the Holy Spirit coming from Christ, our God. They guide and correct us, keeping us living true to the way of Christ that is found in the Scriptures.

Many people will reject my concerns for them, believing that they personally accept all the different denominations. But do you accept your Catholic brothers and sisters, or do you judge them unworthy of forgiveness? And if we accept Catholics as God's children, what is our thinking toward Jehovah's Witnesses, Mormons, and Jewish and Islamic lovers of God? Jesus is the way, the truth, and the life and no one comes to the Father except through faith in Christ, and by showing their relationship in obedience. When we preach the truth and it is not done in love, it is no longer God's truth that we preach, because God's truth is love. Impatience, anger, and unkindness are not among the fruit of the Spirit, and we need to first get honest with ourselves before we begin to try to preach an impatient, angry, and unkind God to people. I have sinned against many people by doing this. God wants us to know his truth, and to gently and kindly share it with others out of a loving attitude, humbly acknowledging that we too are sinners and only God is good.

All of us are wrong in our knowledge of God's truth to some degree. All of us need to re-open the Scriptures and, with the Holy Spirit at our side, be taught more correctly by him. If a person believes in God and is trying to please and honour him, they deserve our respect, for we too are believers in the Most High God. Whereas arrogance, impatience, and disrespect build barriers that separate and divide people, humility, patience, and love help people to listen to what we know, because they know we care.

LET GOD HELP SOW HIS SEED

I recall a lovely Buddhist man who learned written and spoken English from me by reading and discussing the Bible. God, Jesus, and the Bible were new terms to him. I helped him understand the significance of Adam and Eve, their sin, Abraham, Moses, Christ, and the church, before taking him through the gospel of Luke and then the Book of Acts. I explained how the Bible was written and how it came to be here for us today. As he read and we discussed the meaning, I made him feel welcome to disagree. He told me that he did not believe in God or Christ and that he thought the Bible was fiction, but our friendship grew closer anyway. As he read Luke's record of events, I would ask and he would tell me that he didn't believe it. Then I would say something like, "That's okay, but Luke believed it, and I believe it." Many weeks passed and I prayed that God would give me the best, simple explanations to help him understand and believe. He started asking more questions, such as, "Why did God create Satan?" and I would ask God for simple answers. He read about Christ's forgiveness and about heaven.

He was greatly impacted by hearing that God wanted his children with him in his home in heaven. God told me to tell him about all the personal communication that was happening between God and me, and how much he is loved by God, so I told him. I also told him that, because God communicates, I know he and Christ are alive, and I know the Bible is true. I also told him some of the amazing things that God had done in my life, and that some of his "lucky" escapes from certain death were not luck, but the protection of God. I told him that the reason he saw the newspaper ad, and was improving his English with me, was because God loves him and wants him in his family.

One day, as we sat reading and discussing, he suddenly became very distressed and tears started streaming down his face. I felt terrible and asked if I had said something that offended him. He explained that he now believed the Bible and wanted to become a Christian, and he was crying because he knew his father would cry when he hears he is a Christian and not a Buddhist. Without delay, I baptised him into Christ in his backyard swimming pool. He was so excited to know that he was now in Christ, with his sins washed away, that he was born again into God's family, that we were now brothers, and that he was now a Christian and should worship with God's family. It was a very exciting and joy-filled day for all of us.

He went to a church that preached in his language. After church, he chatted to a well-meaning Christian lady who, upon hearing he was a new Christian, listed off things he could never do again, which, according to her, included the sin of drinking alcohol. Why are we so zealous to teach rules and doctrines of men as if they were commands of God? I explained to him that the Bible is clear that Jesus, the Jews, and the Christians drank alcohol, except for some individuals, like John the Baptist, whom God commanded not to drink. I told him that the sin is in getting drunk. We enjoyed sharing a bourbon or a beer together. Then, in May 2012, God commanded me to stop drinking alcohol and, even though I argued with him about it, I couldn't change his decision. God explained that I must stop drinking alcohol because of things in the unseen realm that were deeper than I could understand. I obeyed.

If we know our Bible, and are in close relationship and in consultation with God, then God's maximum blessings can flow from our teaching, encouraging, or correcting. Without God, even if we know our Bible and have the most sincere motives, we can, unwittingly, be like a bull in a china shop in comparison to the finesse of God. God is the master gardener, while we are like goats that eat all the buds and then complain of having no beautiful flowers. We do not give a child a book on how to be an adult, tell them to read it and, after they have read it, expect them to be an adult and punish them if they do not behave like one. Neither has God done that to us. Jesus is the good shepherd, God is the best Father, and they understand that there is a lot of difference between knowing and doing. It sometimes takes time.

LOVE THEM BACK TO LIFE

We all sin more than we know. We are all good at doing bad and bad at doing good. We want to be so much better than we are, but we are weak. God understands, and Jesus sympathises and has died for our sins. Surely we can extend to others, just as generously, the great kindness, patience, and sympathy that God and Christ extend to us. When we have the mind of Christ, we will have the heart of Christ. Until then, we have work to do on ourselves, as we are guided and encouraged by the Holy Spirit. The good company of the Holy Spirit, with his wise instruction and power, will help us to sin less and less, and live a life that pleases God and Christ more and more.

As Christians, all of us need to remind ourselves daily that God is not only loving, but God describes himself as love. Therefore, if we are to change and become more like the nature of our Father, our chief characteristic will become love.

In light of the fact that churches worldwide, in general, have become known far more for splits, for disputes, and for being judgemental and condemning, let's remind ourselves of a few verses from Christianity 101. John 15:10 and 12 say, "If you obey my commands, you remain in my love, just as I have obeyed the Father's commands and remain in his love. My command is this: Love each other as I have loved you." 1 John 4:16-17 says, "And so we know and rely on the love God has for us. God is love. Whoever lives in love lives in God, and God in him. In this way, love is made complete among us so that we will have confidence on the day of judgement, because in this world we are like him."

Jesus commands us to love as he has loved. But taking one look at the world, or one glance at the church, it is evident that we have failed to love as Christ commanded us. We have sinned, we need to repent and humbly seek God's forgiveness. Generally, Christ's church worldwide is deluged with worldly love, typified by "be nice to those who are nice to you, and be kind to those who agree with you," which is not at all God's love or Christ's love. Love is of such high importance in God's family that, without God and Christ loving us enough to die for us, we are dead in our sins. Yet we have not loved others as God and Christ love us. Sadly, we are accomplished at acting like we love; yet we are horrible to anyone who is different—anyone who dares to disagree with us. We use Scripture to justify our judgemental and condemning actions, so we will never change because we are "right" and have the verses to prove it. Meanwhile, our churches are filled with cold shoulders, raised noses, clay-faced expressions that advertise so well that our hearts, our minds, and our attitudes are wrong. Before we correct another person, let's get with the Holy Spirit and allow ourselves to be corrected. Christ is alive, but his love has fled his churches. Christ is in our churches in word, but not in deed.

When I was young, I had long hair, rode a motorbike, wore a leather jacket and had holes in my jeans. I visited two local churches because my heart was aching for the love of Jesus. The greetings I received took the form of silence accompanied by looks and expressions that screamed, "WHAT ARE YOU DOING HERE? GET OUT!" I never returned to those churches and it took a while to get over that "slap in the face." Our own rules of acceptability do not sit well with God because Christ knows my sins and yours, and everyone's sins sent him to the cross. How dare we hold back God's love from a person, when God is so generous in loving all of us? Have we learned nothing? If we read the Scriptures just one time, we will discover warning after warning directed at us and our petty, divisive hearts that want to determine who is welcome and who is not. We put our own eternity on the line when we behave without compassion and kindness.

There are some lovely churches across the planet, headed up by folks who are in touch with the heart of God. They love. They do not have a perfect message, and they need to correct that, but they are preaching and living God's love and Christ's love, and their congregations are exploding. So many people are hurting and aching to be loved—to be accepted. A lot of Christians who are filling up large, fast-growing churches have been hurt by other churches. Some of them are new to God and Christ, and encounter all the love they have longed for, looked for, and never thought existed. When churches have the Jesus touch, there is love and a lot of growth. Praise God for those lovers of God and lovers of souls who are leading churches in the way of love. They are leading people back to Christ and to his way—imperfectly, needing some correction—but when they begin in love, they begin with God's Spirit, and not the spirit that sees the majority of churches, particularly in the western world, dying and wasting away to the degree of being almost dead, instead of being abundantly alive.

With the fields jam packed and so ripe for harvest, we can get so picky that we might choose between ripeness and rightness amongst the crop. We sow seed that is not our own. We must remember that brothers and sisters won to the Lord are not bought by us but by the blood of Christ. We must take great care to not sow a seed that God and Christ would not sow. We must also beware of growing the lambs of God and Christ on spiritual nourishment that falls short of that which the good shepherd would give to them. With the Holy Spirit at our side, we can accurately remove the teaching of men and lift up the true Word of God. We all need correcting. We have all gone off track. God has not asked the impossible. He gives a light to our path along the way, if we will not turn to our own understanding, but listen to the Holy Spirit every step of the way.

The outpouring of the Holy Spirit in the first century saw explosive growth in the church. God is calling us back to his power, which is the only power that achieves explosive, spiritual revival. The very best we can ever be on our own is not good enough; it has never been good enough, and it never will be good enough. The very best we can be could land us in hell because it is not good enough to land us in heaven. To deserve to go to heaven, you have to be as good as God, and you and I are not as good as God. To go to heaven, we need our unrighteousness covered over by the righteousness of Jesus Christ, who is God, and whose home has always been heaven. So it is the perfect life of Christ that gets us to heaven. In a similar way, to please God on earth, and to perfectly achieve all that he has for us to do, takes Christ living in us and living out of us. The Holy Spirit does this for us, if we listen and do what he tells us. God does not just want us to spiritually survive, but he plans for you and me to spiritually thrive.

On Saturday, June 1, 2013, God surprised me by telling me, "You are my champion!" and Gideon immediately came to mind. I could be regarded as an idiot, a liar, or a nut to everyone else, but when God says you are, or you will be, his champion, it changes how you think about yourself. When God talks you up, you rise up. You step into the bigger shoes he gives you, confidently knowing you will grow into them. You put on the larger armour, assured in the knowledge that it is God's armour for you, and you will grow into it.

I think there is something to be gained by comparing the work of the Holy Spirit in our life to that of a personal trainer. If we are into aerobics, circuit training, running, sports, weights, etc., and we use a personal trainer or a coach, we know that the result is much more beneficial than learning skills from a book, or self-learning based on our personal enthusiasm and interest. The personal trainer and coach will teach us the correct way the activity is to be performed, so we do not practise bad habits. A personal trainer will drive us beyond the point we would drive ourselves. We grow, and develop, and achieve our very best much sooner. In fact, we will most likely never be at our best without expert, personal training. The difference between training alone or doing our own thing, and using a professional, personal trainer or coach is enormous. This is why God and Christ have given us the Holy Spirit as our personal trainer and coach. He will teach us and push us to our very best. If we listen to him, we will win the prize—

we will be in the arms of our God eternally. He knows the way and he is faithful to lead us there!

At worship last year, while a preacher was speaking about Joseph, God asked me what was most important about Joseph's life. I said I didn't know, and God told me the most important thing was that his life was written in God's book in heaven. Joseph's life was God's will and that was important. Joseph's life was backed by God's power and that is why Joseph achieved God's purpose for his life. God was reminding me that, if I make my own plans, choose my own path, and go my own way, I can only work in my own strength. However, if I wait for God to reveal his plans, I will have his power; so his plans will achieve his purpose. How much more so is this true for his church? God's will is to have one church—one bride—and his power will make it happen! Many who witnessed the Christ on earth didn't believe because of their man-made traditions and preconceptions. Today, we can be sure that many will not listen and prepare for Christ's return. God has not been sloppy about the way in which he has written his Word. His Word is his best and perfect will for us, but we have been sloppy about the way we read it, learn it, and do it. When we are sloppy with the truth of God, with his Word, we are doing things the hard way. We are missing the power and blessings that God has for those who choose to trust him and do it the way he tells us to do it.

Satan tries to cut us down to a size that poses no threat to him, and often he uses people in the world to ridicule us and put us down. Sadly, he also has lots of volunteers amongst our Christian brothers and sisters who, unwittingly, do some of his dirty work in our lives. God is doing the opposite. God wants to raise us up to be fearless in his army of saints. God wants to give us a new name, and he wants to tell us who we really are, and who we are going to be in his kingdom. But how can God tell us if we cannot hear him? How will we ever hear him, if we do not spend a lot of one-on-one time getting close to him and seeking to please him?

My hope is that God's truth, that he has revealed through me, will pierce your soul, and in the loving hands of the Holy Spirit, you will grow to be a mighty revolutionary, a brave reformer, and a loving leader for the transformation into a new, first century church—preparing the bride to be fit for the soon returning King of Kings, the Lord Jesus Christ, our mighty God and Saviour. God's blessings to all as we show our love through our obedience, and as we reveal our heart through our passion for intimacy with our God, who is completely, madly, and irresistibly in love with us!

BELIEVE GOD'S PLAN
FOR HIS CHURCH

Adam and Eve listened to Satan. Although they were already in God's perfect and handmade paradise, Satan told them lies that amounted to God being mean and not loving, being small and insecure, not being infinitely powerful, and holding them back from the very best.

For all the damage that Satan did to God's perfect creation, and because God saw it coming from the beginning, God devised a perfect plan to undo all of Satan's evil. So today, the Lord Jesus Christ is lifted high and glorified. Because we are broken and see our deep need, and since we see no solution anywhere else, we run into God's arms for our healing. The devil lost because he did not love God, he did not know God, and he did not believe God. He doubted God and didn't take God's Word seriously. The devil thought he knew better, and could do better, by defying God and going his own way. There is no better way. The devil still breathes his God-defying spirit into us. But God has replaced the devil's lies with perfect truth. God has a plan to take us to paradise with him forever. Christ's sacrifice infinitely overpaid our sin debts owed to God, making us free to live—now and always. Christ's church is God's community on earth that preaches good news, relieves suffering, and glorifies God and Christ.

John warns us bluntly in 1 John 2:9-11 that, "Anyone who claims to be in the light but hates his brother is still in the darkness. Whoever loves his brother lives in the light, and there is nothing in him to make him stumble. But whoever hates his brother is in the darkness and walks around in the darkness; he does not know where he is going, because the darkness has blinded him."

None of us want to think that we hate, but when we have negative thoughts that do not lift up a brother or sister—when our thinking about someone is not the way God, Christ, and the Holy Spirit think about our brother or sister—then we do not have thoughts of love for them. And if our thoughts fall short of God's thoughts, we are sinning. If we are comfortable to live with this sin, our spiritual thinking is darkened. God is warning us via John, and we are wise to listen.

Imagine the love someone must have in their heart for you if they are prepared to die for you—to die in your place—and they know their death will follow horrific torture. We are all commanded to be imitators of Christ. And no one imitates Christ without loving others as he loves us. Christ's love is not petty and picky, but forgiving. When we hide envy and jealousy in our heart for a brother or a sister, or have any mean thoughts toward them—whether we act them out or just think them—we have sinned. We do not have the mind and the heart of Christ, and we need to repent and change.

We do not love a brother or a sister with Christ's love when we are only nice to them if they agree with us and are nice to us in return, but if they do not agree with us, we do not like them. Our sinful human nature so easily judges and condemns others; then we excuse ourselves. But what we do to our brothers and sisters, we do to our God.

OUR love covers a multitude of OUR sins. God and Christ are generous and forgiving toward us, and we must be the same to others. Anything less puts our relationship with our God and our Christ at risk. If we think we can have a warm, cosy, close relationship with God, and cultivate mean thoughts about brothers and sisters, we urgently need to read the Scriptures because we are greatly mistaken.

If we use the Scriptures to justify being mean, and talking about people behind their backs, and undermining them, we need to be honest with the Scriptures and, under the guidance of the Holy Spirit, take our heart and our challenges to love others before our God. Many people are very challenging to love. It is difficult to have genuine love in our heart for people who are selfish, nasty, dishonest, and mean; but every time we sin, we are being selfish, nasty, dishonest, and mean to our God and to our Christ—yet we are greatly loved by them.

God is easy to love because he is so loving and kind. God is never mean and nasty. However, God does get blunt and says it like it is, just like we read in Scripture. If we are ugly of heart, we are likely to hear him tell us that we are ugly of heart. But at the very same time, God's love for us can be felt. Sometimes God is very confronting, but he is never like one shouting abuse from afar. Rather, he is like one holding us in his arms, sitting us on his knee, cuddling us, and appealing to us to change. God is always motivated by love for us—for all people. He is never hateful.

Do we love God and each other like Christ did? Christ loved his Father, his enemies the Pharisees, his enemies the Romans, and you, and me, and everyone. The Roman flogging ended before it killed Jesus, to prolong his death and agony on the cross. Jesus denied us nothing—his blood of life included.

Today, the whole world, including the church, is dying for Christ's love. Christ's divine, loving nature set him apart from being an ordinary man. As imitators of Christ, we too are set apart from being ordinary men and women, if the divine nature—the Holy Spirit—is at work within us.

We must learn to be like God, which is impossible for us if we try to do it alone. However, we have the power of the Holy Spirit to help us, if we ask for it. If all we are using is our own effort, then what we call love will be not much better than what God calls hate. When the disciples were running on their own power, they envied each other, were suspicious and jealous of each other, and did not love each other. But with the power and guidance of the Holy Spirit, they were very different men; they had the mind of Christ and did not gratify their carnal nature.

Churches in the first century had troubles whenever they lived independently of the Holy Spirit. The struggles within and between our churches today result from our independence from the Holy Spirit, and the solution is dependence on him. Our churches are different and, if they are not in overt contention, potential struggles are just below the surface. There is only one Holy Spirit and his way is one of harmony. If the Holy Spirit had seen a benefit for many churches, he would have started many churches.

Instead, the Holy Spirit founded one church and calls us back to one church. The question is no longer who is correct, or which is the correct church, because all fail the truth test. The way is found in the Holy Spirit. Try to navigate the narrow way of Christ. Leaning on our own understanding has not cast a light down our path. We are all on paths that miss the mark. God intended something easier, happier, clearer and far more powerful for his church, and he calls us back to what he originally intended. No church is as God intended, and that is why he calls us back to the Holy Spirit.

After the first century, we pulled away from God; we thought we knew better than God and went looking for a better way. We didn't find it. We cannot find it on our own. After nearly 2,000 years of trying and failing, God is calling us back to his pattern for the church of his dreams. These are the last of the last days. The Bridegroom comes swiftly. God does not intend to present the bride of Christ—the church—as a dishevelled, bickering mess, but as one harmonious church, unified under the guidance of the Holy Spirit. I pray that God will fill our hearts with Godly sorrow and a spirit of repentance so that we may rejoice together on earth—and very soon in heaven. We are not capable of imagining the manifold change in God's kingdom that will take place when we stop using our power—defined by our carnal nature that hates so naturally—and submit to God's power and the guidance of the Holy Spirit. Christ and God will explode out of it. We will be the "Emmanuels" that we were born to be. It will be God's love revolution.

All of us have added to and taken from God's Scriptures. There is only truth from God or lies from Satan, and when we take or add to Scripture, we end up with some of Satan's lies. God's truth is 100% victorious and positive, but our churches are not 100% victorious and positive because we have unwittingly believed and adopted some of the devil's lies, which he makes seem good, true and harmless. The devil wants to make God look bad and most churches, unwittingly, serve the devil's plan quite well.

We all have a calling from God—a challenging, but very positive and exciting, assignment. It is to draw close to God and Christ, to hear clearly from the Holy Spirit, to stop teaching, practising, and living what is partly man-made, and to become living epistles—people filled with the love and the mind of Christ.

The Scriptures reveal that, in the end times, half the church will be ready for the Bridegroom and half will not be. Their oil will have run out. Choose today to spend more time getting close to God so you will know him personally, intimately. Be filled with the oil of God so that you burn brightly and give off God's light. I hope everyone is ready for the return of Christ.

These final years of Christ's kingdom on earth are going to be so exciting. But hurting people hurt people, and broken people break people. We have all done it and had it done to us. We all need to rush into God's arms for healing because he has huge plans and he wants all of us to play a part in them. We squabble, pick, accuse, and fight like little children, and it is time for the Lord's church to grow up, mature, and prepare herself for her Bridegroom. This is the most positive time on earth, ever!

The devil wants you to believe every reason why you can't, but God knows that, according to his will and his power, you can do more than you can possibly imagine. Yes, the worldwide revival is beginning soon and I hope you will be a stakeholder in it. The church of God's dreams—the radiant bride of Christ—is waking up for the Bridegroom is coming very soon.

As a dad or a mum, if your much-loved son or daughter were getting married, you would do everything possible to ensure their big day was perfect. Similarly, God is preparing us—the church—for the wedding of his Son. We cannot possibly imagine how mind-blowing this celebration will be. The wedding feast and God's plans are bigger than Protestants, bigger than Catholics, bigger than Judaism, bigger than Islam, bigger than any of our religious comfort zones. It is bigger than you and me because this is Christ's big day, the bride's big day, the Father's big day, and nothing and no one is going to spoil it. We must prepare to come together with one heart and one mind—as the one bride of Christ. The devil may have been permitted to spoil quite a few of God's special days, but nothing and no one gets to spoil the wedding feast of Christ. If I never get to see you beforehand, I look forward to seeing you in heaven for the wedding celebration that never ends. God bless you!

MINISTRIES THAT HAVE BLESSED ME SPIRITUALLY

I commend to you those listed below who God has used in person, or their writings, or their sermons, to grow me. None of the listed ministries are perfect and none of the mentioned ministers are perfect. You should always compare all teaching with God's Scriptures and you should ask for the Holy Spirit's guidance in learning what is spiritually profitable for your life.

Every ministry I know falls short of what God likes and wants, as does every minister. This is not to judge or criticise them, but is simply a fact, for we are human and it is only when we are fully in God that we please God fully, and the busy nature of many ministries often results in distance from God rather than closeness to God.

God has blessed my life via many authors, particularly Philip Yancey, Lee Strobel, and Lynn Anderson, and I believe you too will find life-changing blessings from God on the pages of their books.

I must add a special thank you to Senior Pastor Jason Elsmore at Gateway church, Mansfield, Brisbane, our church family and place of worship.

I thank those listed below and on the next page for the manifold blessings!

Lynn Anderson - www.lynnanderson.org
Jason Elsmore & team - www.gatewaybaptist.com.au
Jimmy Evans & team - www.tfc.org
Billy Graham - www.billygraham.org
Craig Groeschel - www.lifechurch.tv
Bill Hybels - www.willowcreek.com
Max Lucado - www.maxlucado.com
Joyce Meyer - www.joycemeyer.org
Robert Morris - www.gatewaypeople.com

Jim McGuiggan - www.jimmcguiggan.com
Joel Osteen - www.joelosteen.com
Jon Reed - www.hilltopchurchofchrist.com
Lee Strobel - www.leestrobel.com
Rick Warren - www.saddleback.com
Shane Willard - www.shanewillardministries.org
Philip Yancey - www.philipyancey.com

You can also find the written works from many of these individuals by visiting www.GoodReads.com and simply entering the authors name in the search box.

Made in the USA
Lexington, KY
09 October 2014